Wrestling's Most

Wanted

Also by Floyd Conner

Football's Most Wanted

Baseball's Most Wanted

Golf!

Fore!

This Date in Sports History

Day by Day in Cincinnati Reds History

Day by Day in Cincinnati Bengals History

Wrestling's Most
Wanted

The Top 10 Book of Pro Wrestling's Outrageous Performers, Punishing Pile Drivers, and Other Oddities

Floyd Conner

Brassey's

WASHINGTON, D.C.

Library of Congress Cataloging-in-Publication Data

Conner, Floyd, 1951–
        Wrestling's most wanted : the top 10 book of pro
wrestling's outrageous performers, punishing pile drivers,
and other oddities / Floyd Conner.
        p.   cm.
Includes bibliographical references and index.
ISBN 1-57488-308-9
1. Wrestlers—United States—Biography. I. Title.

GV1196.A1 C66 2001
796.812'092'273—dc21
[B]
                                                                00-052949

Printed in Canada on acid-free paper that meets
the American National Standards
Institute Z39-48 Standard

Brassey's
22841 Quicksilver Drive
Dulles, Virginia 20166

Designed by Pen & Palette Unlimited

Photographs by Dr. Mike Lano. For more
information, contact wrealano@aol.com

First Edition

10 9 8 7 6 5 4 3 2 1

Contents

List of Photographs

Introduction

Each year more than 20 million fans attend professional wrestling matches. Millions more watch the events on pay-per-view. Professional wrestling programs are consistently among the most highly rated on cable television.

Wrestling's Most Wanted honors professional wrestling's outstanding offenders. This book contains top-ten lists of the wildest matches, deadliest holds, and most outrageous performers in wrestling history. The lists feature the most outlandish gimmicks, sneakiest managers, craziest fans, dirtiest wrestlers, and the sexiest women in wrestling.

Nothing is too outrageous for professional wrestling. Morgus the Maniac was led to the ring in a straightjacket. Tricky Ricki Starr was a wrestling ballet dancer. Darren Drozdov was called "Puke" because of his unique ability to vomit on command. Leatherface claimed that his mask was made from the faces of defeated foes. The Gargoyle liked to lick and sniff the feet of his opponents.

In this book you'll meet Amish Roadkill, the Angry Amish Chickenplucker. Stamp Lickage, a disgruntled postal employee-turned-wrestler, delivers pain to his opponents. Frenchy Riviera is a 440-pound wrestler who claimed he was formerly a male stripper on the French Riviera. Gangrel wears fangs and pours buckets of blood on his opponents.

Some of today's superstars had humble beginnings. Hunter Hearst Helmsley, a three-time World Wrestling Federation champion, began his career as Terra Rizing. Glenn Jacobs, the wrestler behind the mask of Kane, was once known as The Christmas Creature, Santa's largest elf. Kevin Nash may be "Big Sexy" today, but in a past wrestling life, he was Oz, a silver-haired wizard. The Ultimate Warrior used to be known as The Rock, and The Rock was once known as Flex Cavana.

Professional wrestling is no longer the "wrasslin" of years past. It has become sports entertainment. Film actors and television stars have competed in professional wrestling matches. Scrawny actor David Arquette actually won the World Championship Wrestling heavyweight title. Mr. T, the actor who starred in television's *The A-Team,* wrestled in the main event of the first Wrestlemania. Jay Leno, host of *The Tonight Show,* teamed with Diamond Dallas Page to defeat Hulk Hogan and Eric Bischoff. In the early 1980s, comedian Andy Kaufman carried on a feud with wrestler Jerry "The King" Lawler.

In recent years, pro wrestling has taken on a sexier image. Sable, a former WWF women's champion, has appeared on the cover of *Playboy.* Kimberly, wife of Diamond Dallas Page, was also featured in a *Playboy* pictorial. Sunny, a manager of wrestling champions, has had more than a million of her photos downloaded on the Internet. Debra McMichael, another WWF Women's champion, was a former Miss Illinois and Miss Texas USA.

Wrestlers often achieve success in other fields. Jesse "The Body" Ventura, one of wrestling's most colorful characters, was elected governor of Minnesota in 1998. Rowdy Roddy

Piper has starred in more than twenty films. Bill Goldberg is just one of many wrestlers who played professional football. Manager Jimmy Hart was a member of a sixties pop group, The Gentrys.

This book introduces you to nearly 700 of wrestling's most-wanted grapplers. Their offenses range from bad makeup to outrageous gimmicks. Be on the lookout for these individuals.

Entertaining Entrances

A wrestling match begins long before the wrestlers enter the ring. Today, wrestlers have their own entrance music. As they walk to the ring, their images are projected on a Jumbotron, often accompanied by pyrotechnic displays. Sometimes the entrances last as long as the matches. The following wrestlers knew how to make an entrance.

1. THE ULTIMATE WARRIOR

Few wrestlers generated as much excitement on their way to the ring as The Ultimate Warrior. Unlike most wrestlers, who walk to the ring slowly to get a response from the crowd, the Warrior ran down the aisle at full speed. Once in the ring, he grabbed the ropes and shook them like a madman. Before the match even started, the crowd was usually in a frenzy. The Warrior's ultimate moment came on April 1, 1990, when he defeated Hulk Hogan at Wrestlemania VI to win the World Wrestling Federation (WWF) title.

2. STING

For the past decade, Sting has been one of the most popular and successful wrestlers in World Championship Wrestling

(WCW). Sting often used the element of surprise in his entrances. Roaming the arena rafters like a Phantom of the Opera, he would unexpectedly lower himself to the ring on a cable. On one occasion, it appeared that the cable had broken, and Sting had fallen to the mat. Happily, it was just a hoax staged by Hollywood Hogan, and the body turned out to be a dummy. The stunt eerily foreshadowed the tragic fall which took the life of Owen Hart in May 1999.

3. CHRIS JERICHO

In 1999, Chris Jericho made the move from WCW to the WWF. His WWF debut in Chicago was one of the most spectacular in wrestling history. As Jericho stood on the ramp leading to the ring, a millennium clock on the big screen behind him ticked down to Y2J. The Y2K crisis never lived up to the hype, but Y2J did, becoming a major player in the WWF in the year 2000.

4. GORGEOUS GEORGE

Gorgeous George was wrestling's first great showman. He was the man wrestling fans loved to hate. Dressed in a frilly robe, "The Human Orchid" strutted to the ring to the strains of "Pomp and Circumstance." His valet used an atomizer to spray the ring and the opponent with a fragrance named "George No. 4." Fans at ringside were handed gold-plated "Georgie" hairpins. His outrageous antics were so effective that boxing legend Muhammad Ali admitted that his persona was influenced by Gorgeous George.

5. THE GORILLA

Cage matches are common in professional wrestling today, but a popular wrestler known as "The Gorilla" used a different approach back in the 1940s: He was wheeled to the ring in a cage. Once inside the ring, his handlers would release him.

6. THE GODFATHER

It's not uncommon for a wrestler to be accompanied to the ring by a sexy woman. The Godfather, wrestling's resident pimp, outdid everyone by arriving each week with a different group of "hos." Before the action began, The Godfather usually offered two of his prized "hos" to his opponent if he agreed to forfeit the match. Many wrestlers, including Dean Malenko, have accepted the offer.

7. THE SANDMAN

A four-time Extreme Championship Wrestling (ECW) champion, The Sandman has always been a fan favorite. Rather than walk down the ramp to the ring, The Sandman usually emerges from the stands with a beer in one hand and a cigarette in the other. His theme music is Metallica's "Enter Sandman."

8. THE BUSHWHACKERS

For years The Sheepherders were one of the most feared and hated tag teams in wrestling. In the early 1990s, they changed their name to The Bushwhackers and became fan favorites in the WWF. Swinging their arms as they marched to the ring, cousins Luke and Butch made The Bushwhacker Stomp their trademark. The zany New Zealanders displayed their mutual affection by licking each other's heads.

9. KOKO B. WARE

Wrestling fans remember Koko B. Ware more for his entrances than for his matches. The former WWF star danced to the ring holding a cockatoo. He was attired in brightly colored outfits and wore outrageous hats.

10. **THE ROAD DOGG**

Jesse James, also known as The Road Dogg, was one of The New Age Outlaws, along with partner "Bad Ass" Billy Gunn. The Outlaws were WWF tag-team champions in the late 1990s, and The Road Dogg won the hardcore championship in 1998. James is known for his ring introductions, which would make any announcer envious. Prior to many of his matches, he introduces himself in a manner reminiscent of famed ring announcer Michael Buffer.

Unmatched Matches

In a normal match, a wrestler can win by pinfall, submission, disqualification, or countout. Promoters discovered that by making a match more dangerous or unusual, they could heighten fan interest. Over the years, many different types of matches have evolved.

1. THE EXPLODING-RING MATCH

Popular in Japan, the use of explosives in wrestling matches has taken the sport to a new level of danger. C-4 explosives are placed throughout the ring, making it a virtual mine field. One misstep can result in serious injury for a wrestler. The exploding ring was featured in a 1995 King of the Death Match tournament won by Cactus Jack.

2. LOSER-GOES-TO-JAIL MATCH

The loser-leaves-town Match has long been a staple of professional wrestling. This kind of match was often staged when a wrestler was about to leave the region to join another federation. In the early 1990s, The Big Boss Man and The Mountie competed in a loser-goes-to-jail match. The Mountie lost and spent a night in the cooler.

3. HELL-IN-THE-CELL MATCH

The cage match is a favorite for settling grudges because of
its brutal nature. Two wrestlers are enclosed in a cage, and
the first one to climb out of the cage or exit through the door
is the winner. The hell-in-the-cell match, created by the
WWF, took the cage match a step further. A sixteen-foot
cage, covered by a roof, was installed for a match between
The Undertaker and Shawn Michaels. The first hell-in-the-cell
match took place at the Kiel Center in St. Louis on October 5,
1997. Despite taking a horrific beating, Michaels won.

4. THE INFERNO-OF-FIRE MATCH

The feud between The Undertaker and Kane is the story of
Cain and Abel with a twist. Supposedly, as a child, The
Undertaker had lived in a mortuary. While playing with
embalming fluids, he accidentally set the house on fire. The
blaze killed his parents and horribly disfigured his brother,
Kane. Kane arrived in the WWF in October 1997, hell-bent
on destroying his brother. At Wrestlemania in 1998, they
met in an inferno-of-fire match. A wall of flames surrounded
the ring and intensified during the match, which The Undertaker won.

5. THE BARBED-WIRE MATCH

Perhaps no contest is more dangerous than a barbed-wire
match. In one infamous example, Abdullah the Butcher and
Dusty Rhodes tore one another to shreds. By the time the
match was stopped, ringside spectators had been splattered
with the participants' blood. The wrestler Sabu has scars all
over his body, reminders of his barbed-wire matches.
Hardcore icon Terry Funk even competed in flaming-barbed-
wire matches.

6. THE SICILIAN-STRETCHER MATCH

In a death match, the action continues until one contestant is incapacitated. For instance, the Texas death match ends when one of the wrestlers is unable to get up before a ten count. One of the most dramatic death matches is the Sicilian-stretcher match, in which the loser is carried out of the ring on a stretcher.

7. BATTLE ROYAL

A longtime favorite of wrestling fans is the battle royal. The battle royal begins with the ring full of wrestlers and ends when just one remains. The object of the battle royal is to throw your opponent over the top rope. Andre the Giant claimed he never lost a battle royal.

8. THE LADDER MATCH

In recent years, the ladder match has become popular. A ladder is placed in the middle of the ring with something, usually a title belt, suspended above it. The first to climb the ladder and grab the belt wins. One of the most memorable ladder matches was the intercontinental title Match between Razor Ramon and Shawn Michaels at Wrestlemania X in 1994. Ramon won the match and the title. In 2000, Justin Credible successfully defended his ECW world title in a stair-way-to-hell match against Tommy Dreamer. In that contest, barbed wire was placed atop the ladder.

9. THE DOG-COLLAR CHAIN MATCH

As the name suggests, a dog-collar chain match requires each wrestler to wear a dog collar around his neck. The collars are linked by a chain that the wrestlers often use as a weapon. A particularly brutal and bloody dog-collar match

occurred in the early 1980s when Roddy Piper defeated Greg
Valentine.

10. THE EVENING-GOWN MATCH

In order to showcase the sex appeal of women wrestlers, the
WWF created the evening-gown match. In this match and its
variations, scantily clad women wrestle until one has torn off
most of her opponent's clothes. At that point, she is declared
the victor, although the audience tends to be the real winner. In 2000, Daffney and Ms. Hancock, who were fighting
for the affections of David Flair, engaged in a wedding-gown
match.

Celebrity Wrestlers

Professional wrestling now categorizes itself as "sports entertainment." When Wrestlemania was introduced in 1985, WWF owner Vince McMahon hired celebrities to be special attractions at the event, a tradition that continues to this day. Actors, athletes, musicians, and television personalities have participated in professional wrestling as wrestlers, referees, announcers, managers, and timekeepers.

1. DAVID ARQUETTE

Actor David Arquette starred in the wrestling movie *Ready to Rumble,* which featured WCW wrestlers. In April 2000, while promoting the movie on a WCW television broadcast, Arquette became involved in a tag-team match. He teamed with Diamond Dallas Page against Eric Bischoff and world champion Jeff Jarrett. According to the rules of the match, the winner would be declared champion. Arquette pinned Bischoff and became the only actor crowned a wrestling world champion.

2. **ANDY KAUFMAN**

No celebrity ever became more obsessed with wrestling than comedian Andy Kaufman. During his appearances on *Saturday Night Live,* Kaufman outraged many viewers by wrestling women. Declaring himself The Intergender Champion, he defeated more than three hundred women. On April 5, 1982, Kaufman was hospitalized with a neck injury after wrestler Jerry "The King" Lawler used an illegal pile driver on him. The feud between the two escalated, and Kaufman declared that he would get out of the wrestling business if Lawler agreed to be his partner in a tag-team match. It turned out to be a trick as Kaufman threw powder into Lawler's eyes. Kaufman's mentor was wrestling great Fred Blassie. They co-starred in a short film, *My Breakfast with Blassie,* a takeoff on the movie *My Dinner with Andre.*

3. **MR. T**

Mr. T is best known for his role as B.A. Barracus on the television series *The A-Team* and as the mohawked boxer Clubber Lang in *Rocky III.* He became a part of wrestling history when he teamed with Hulk Hogan in the main event of the first Wrestlemania. Hogan and Mr. T defeated Paul Orndorff and Roddy Piper. Mr. T also wrestled Roddy Piper at Wrestlemania II in a match in which Piper was disqualified.

4. **JAY LENO**

Jay Leno has frequently hosted wrestlers such as Bret Hart and Hulk Hogan on *The Tonight Show.* In 1998, he agreed to enter the ring after Eric Bischoff repeatedly made fun of Leno's comedy monologues on WCW broadcasts. Leno and Diamond Dallas Page teamed up against Bischoff and

Hogan. With the help of some outside interference, Leno was able to pin Bischoff.

5. CYNDI LAUPER

Cyndi Lauper was an integral part of the rock 'n' roll connection, which helped popularize wrestling in the mid-1980s. One of the most successful women rock performers of the 1980s, Lauper had two number-one hits, "Time After Time" and "True Colors." Wrestling manager Captain Lou Albano appeared as her father in the video for "Girls Just Want to Have Fun." Lauper made many appearances on WWF broadcasts and even managed Wendi Richter when she won the women's championship belt from Leilani Kai at Wrestlemania I.

6. MUHAMMAD ALI

Three-time heavyweight boxing champion Muhammad Ali is considered by many to be the greatest boxer of all time. On June 25, 1976, he decided to test his skills against Japanese wrestling champion Antonio Inoki in a match held in Tokyo. The 15-round bout was declared a draw, but it should have been a no-contest as Inoki spent the entire time retreating about the mat in a crab position. Ali also refereed the main event at Wrestlemania I.

7. DENNIS RODMAN

Basketball's bad boy Dennis Rodman decided to settle his on-the-court feud with Utah Jazz forward Karl Malone in the wrestling ring. At the WCW Bash at the Beach pay-per-view in July 1998, Rodman teamed with Hollywood Hogan against Malone and partner Diamond Dallas Page.

8. PETE ROSE

Baseball's all-time hit leader Pete Rose is one of the many celebrities to appear on the Wrestlemania broadcasts. It has become an annual tradition for Rose to be rendered unconscious by a wrestler, usually Kane. When asked why he would agree to suffer this indignity every year, Rose replied that at least he wasn't banned from wrestling.

9. MORTON DOWNEY, JR.

Morton Downey, Jr. was the host of a popular confrontational talk show in the late 1980s. The controversial host met his match when he was interviewed by Roddy Piper at Wrestlemania in 1989. Piper asked Downey to put out his cigarette, and when he refused, Piper put it out with a fire extinguisher, spraying Downey as he writhed on the canvas.

10. LIBERACE

Flamboyant pianist Liberace seems an unlikely participant in a wrestling event, but at Wrestlemania I, he was the celebrity timekeeper.

Going Hollywood

Professional wrestlers have appeared in dozens of Hollywood movies, and not just as wrestlers. Some of the matmen to grace the big screen include King Kong Bundy, Tricky Ricki Starr, The Haiti Kid, Captain Lou Albano, Bill Goldberg, and Diamond Dallas Page.

1. ROWDY RODDY PIPER

Rowdy Roddy Piper has starred in more than twenty action films. His biggest hit, *They Live,* directed by John Carpenter, was number one at the box office in its initial week of release in 1988. In the film, Piper played a drifter who tries to stop an alien invasion. Piper uttered the immortal line, "I'm here to chew gum and kick butt, and I'm all out of gum." Other Piper films include *Hell Comes to Frogtown* and *Buy and Cell.* He also starred in a television pilot with Jesse Ventura in which they played former professional wrestlers-turned-detectives.

2. HOLLYWOOD HOGAN

As one of the most popular wrestlers in history, Hulk Hogan inevitably attracted the attention of Hollywood. He first gained national attention with his role as Thunderlips in *Rocky III* in 1982. Two years later Hogan won the WWF world title when he defeated the Iron Sheik. Hogan has appeared in a number of films including *Suburban Commando, Santa with Muscles, No Holds Barred, Spy Hard,* and *Gremlins III.* When he moved to WCW in 1994, he changed his name to Hollywood Hogan to reflect his celebrity stature. Hogan also starred in the action television series *Thunder in Paradise.*

3. JESSE VENTURA

Jesse Ventura first gained fame as a wrestler and later with his improbable victory in the 1998 Minnesota gubernatorial race. In between his wrestling and political careers, Ventura appeared in several films. His most memorable role was as a SWAT team member battling an invisible alien in the 1987 film *Predator.* His most memorable line, "I ain't got time to bleed," became the title of his autobiography. Ventura also starred in another Arnold Schwarzenegger film, *The Running Man,* and was hilarious as a play-by-play announcer in *Repossessed,* a parody of *The Exorcist.*

4. PROFESSOR TORU TANAKA

Professor Toru Tanaka was a top Japanese wrestler in the 1960s and 1970s. A three-time WWF tag-team champion with Mr. Fuji, Tanaka won many matches by throwing salt into his opponents' eyes. In the 1980s, Tanaka appeared as the butler in *Pee Wee's Big Adventure* and as a martial-arts expert in *An Eye for an Eye.*

5. TOR JOHNSON

Tor Johnson was a professional wrestler before beginning a career in horror films. The nearly 400-pound Johnson is best known for his roles in the movies of Ed Wood, often considered the worst director of all time. Johnson played Lobo, the dim-witted assistant to a mad scientist in *Bride of the Monster* (1956). His most famous role is as the police inspector-turned-alien-controlled zombie in Wood's bad film classic, *Plan Nine from Outer Space* (1959). Johnson also had a starring role as a man transformed into a monster by an A-bomb blast in the dreadful *Beast of Yucca Flats* (1961).

6. GEORGE "THE ANIMAL" STEELE

When director Tim Burton made the film *Ed Wood* in 1994, there was only one man who could play Tor Johnson: wrestling wild man George "The Animal" Steele. With his bald head and hairy body, Steele was a dead ringer for Johnson.

7. OX BAKER

At six feet, five inches tall and 300 pounds, Ox Baker was an imposing figure in the ring. His fearsome appearance landed him the role of a lethal wrestler in John Carpenter's cult classic, *Escape from New York* (1981). Near the end of the film, Baker is matched against Snake Plissken (played by Kurt Russell) in a battle to the death.

8. TERRY FUNK

A professional wrestling legend, Terry Funk is still going strong in his mid-fifties. Funk had featured roles in two Sylvester Stallone films, *Over the Top* (1987) and *Paradise Alley* (1978), in which he played Frankie the Thumper.

9. ANDRE THE GIANT

For years Andre the Giant was literally pro wrestling's biggest attraction. He proved that he was effective on the big screen as well. His best-loved role was as Fezzik in the 1987 film *The Princess Bride.*

10. TIGER CHUNG LEE

Tiger Chung Lee was a WWF star in the early 1980s. His imposing presence made him an ideal villain in films such as *The Golden Child* (1986), starring Eddie Murphy, and *Red Head* (1988), starring Arnold Schwarzenegger.

Music to Their Ears

*S*ince the early 1980s, music has played an important role in professional wrestling. A match between WWF champion Hulk Hogan and challenger Roddy Piper received the highest ratings of any show ever aired on MTV. Before he became a wrestler, Hogan was a bass player in a rock band. The Scot, Piper, used to play bagpipes before a match, and once broke one of Cyndi Lauper's platinum records over Captain Lou Albano's head. In 2000, Billy Corgan of The Smashing Pumpkins made several appearances during ECW matches.

1.   THE HOnKY TONK MAN

The Honky Tonk Man, with his muttonchops and ornate jumpsuits, was wrestling's answer to Elvis Presley. If his singing didn't disable an opponent, he usually resorted to hitting him over the head with a guitar. The Honky Tonk Man won the WWF intercontinental title in June 1987 and successfully defended it for a record fourteen months.

2. **THE DISCO INFERNO**

Disco isn't dead, at least not to The Disco Inferno. The Inferno entered the ring wearing silk shirts, tight pants, and gold chains. Though a capable wrestler, he's no threat to John Travolta as a dancer. A high point in his career came in 1997 when he won the WCW television title. Some of his finishing moves include The Chart Buster, Last Dance, and The Boogie Oogie Oogie.

3. **THE MAESTRO**

Not to be confused with the character on *Seinfeld,* The Maestro brought a little culture to professional wrestling. The piano-playing grappler was accompanied to the ring by his lovely blonde assistant, Symphony. Before he assumed the role of The Maestro in the late 1990s, the blonde wrestler was known as Gorgeous George III.

4. **ROCK & ROLL BUCK ZUM HOFE**

A star in the early 1980s, Rock & Roll Buck Zum Hofe was one of the first wrestlers to have rock music played during his entrance. Often he carried a boom box to the ring. He defeated Mike Graham for the American Wrestling Association light-heavyweight championship.

5. **THE ROCK n ROLL EXPRESS**

Robert Gibson and Ricky Morton formed a tag team known as The Rock n Roll Express. Between 1985 and 1987, they held the National Wrestling Alliance world tag-team title on four different occasions.

6. JEFF JARRETT

During his stint as Double J in the World Wrestling Federation, Jeff Jarrett declared himself the greatest living country singer, a claim not substantiated by his vocal performances in the ring. His matches often ended when he bashed his opponent over the head with his guitar.

7. CURT HENNIG

Curt Hennig won the AWA world title from Nick Bockwinkel in May 1987. A decade later, while in the WCW, he formed his own country music band. His single, "Rap Is Crap," infuriated Konnan, who had recorded his own rap song.

8. JIMMY HART

Manager extraordinaire Jimmy Hart frequently wears ties decorated with musical notes or piano keys. Hart was a member of a Memphis-based group, The Gentrys, who recorded a top-five hit, "Keep on Dancing," in 1965.

9. JESSE VENTURA

After conquering the worlds of professional wrestling, acting, and politics, Jesse Ventura has now set his sights on Broadway. In 2000, it was announced that a musical based on his life, tentatively titled *The Body Ventura,* was about to go into production. In the 1980s, Ventura recorded a rock song titled "The Body Rules." He was so proud of the record that he speculated that the Rolling Stones might someday be his opening act.

10. **THE SLAMMYS**

The WWF began releasing albums featuring wrestlers and their theme songs in the 1980s. Shortly thereafter, an annual award show, *The Slammys,* honored the top performers. The event usually resulted in a melee between winners and sore losers.

From the NFL to the WWF

Before stepping into the ring, many wrestlers have already made a name for themselves in professional football. Kevin Greene, an All-Pro linebacker and one of the NFL's all-time leaders in sacks, made frequent appearances as a wrestler in the WCW. Brian Pillman played for the Cincinnati Bengals before turning to professional wrestling. Other former NFL players who have entered the squared circle include Alex Karras, William "The Refrigerator" Perry, Mark Gastineau, Walter Johnson, Ron Pritchard, Jim Covert, Russ Francis, Ernie Holmes, Bill Fralic, and Harvey Martin.

1. BRONKO NAGURSKI

Bronko Nagurski holds the distinction of being the only man to win a wrestling world title and be elected to the Pro Football Hall of Fame. Nagurski played fullback, linebacker, and tackle for the Chicago Bears between 1930 and 1943. Nagurski was known as one of the hardest hitters in football history. He used his power to defeat Lou Thesz in 1939 to win the National Wrestling Alliance world belt. Two years later, Nagurski won the belt a second time. His signature move was a flying block.

2. LEO NOMELLINI

Leo "The Lion" Nomellini played both offensive and defensive tackle for the San Francisco Forty-Niners between 1950 and 1963. A ten-time Pro Bowler, he had the distinction of being named All Pro at both defensive and offensive tackle. Despite often playing sixty minutes, he never missed a game. Nomellini became one of the first professional football players to wrestle in the off-season. In the early 1960s, he teamed with both Verne Gagne and Wilbur Snyder to win AWA world tag-team titles.

3. GUS SONNENBERG

Despite weighing less than two hundred pounds, "Dynamite" Gus Sonnenberg was a four-time All-Pro tackle in the 1920s. He was even more impressive as a wrestler. On January 4, 1929, Sonnenberg defeated the legendary Ed "Strangler" Lewis to win the National Wrestling Alliance world title. His finishing move was the flying tackle. He is also credited with inventing the drop kick.

4. WAHOO MCDANIEL

Wahoo McDaniel played linebacker for the Houston Oilers, Denver Broncos, New York Jets, and Miami Dolphins from 1960 to 1968. The two-time All Pro had a long and successful career in wrestling after his retirement from football. McDaniel won the United States wrestling title four times between 1981 and 1984. He also teamed with Mark Youngblood to win the NWA world tag-team title in 1984.

5. ERNIE LADD

Voted All Pro in 1964 and 1965, Ernie "The Cat" Ladd played defensive tackle for San Diego, Houston, and Kansas City from 1961 to 1968. The self-proclaimed "King of Professional Wrestling" won the North American heavyweight title during the 1970s. At six feet, nine inches tall and nearly 320 pounds, "The Big Cat" was an imposing figure on the football field and in the wrestling ring.

6. STEVE MCMICHAEL

Steve "Mongo" McMichael played defensive tackle in the National Football League for fifteen years and was a member of the Super Bowl champion Chicago Bears in 1986. Following his retirement from football, McMichael became a star in the WCW and won the United States belt in 1997.

7. BILL GOLDBERG

Bill Goldberg was an outstanding football player at the University of Georgia before playing nose tackle for the Atlanta Falcons from 1992 to 1994. His rapid rise to stardom in professional wrestling is unparalleled. He began his wrestling career with an unprecedented 173-match win streak which culminated when he defeated Hollywood Hogan for the WCW world title in July 1998.

8. "BIG DADDY" GENE LIPSCOMB

"Big Daddy" Gene Lipscomb was a 290-pound defensive lineman who played for the Los Angeles Rams, Baltimore Colts, and Pittsburgh Steelers between 1953 and 1962. One of the biggest players of his day and surprisingly quick, Lipscomb was a nightmare for NFL halfbacks. Big Daddy wrestled in the off-season and earned nearly three times as much in the ring as he did on the football field.

9. MANNY FERNANDEZ

Manny Fernandez was an outstanding defensive tackle for the Miami Dolphins from 1968 to 1975. Fernandez played for two Super Bowl champions and was a member of the undefeated Dolphins' team of 1972. He has enjoyed a long and successful career in professional wrestling. In October 1984, he teamed with Dusty Rhodes to win the NWA world tag-team title and two years later repeated the feat with Ravishing Rick Rude as his partner. His finishing move is a forearm smash, which he calls The Flying Burrito.

10. LAWRENCE TAYLOR

New York Giants' linebacker Lawrence Taylor is often mentioned as the greatest defensive player in National Football League history. At Wrestlemania XI, Taylor defeated Bam Bam Bigelow in his only wrestling match.

Real Names

Like actors, professional wrestlers assume stage names, or, in this case, mat names. As you might guess, their wrestling monikers tend to be more colorful than the names they were born with.

1. MICHAEL HICKENBOTTOM

If you don't know who Michael Hickenbottom is, think again. He's been a WWF tag-team champion as a member of The Midnight Rockers and with partners Diesel and Stone Cold Steve Austin. He was also the WWF world champion three times between 1996 and 1998. That's right, Michael Hickenbottom is bettter known as "The Heartbreak Kid" Shawn Michaels.

2. TERRY BRUNK

Like Terry Funk, Terry Brunk is a two-time ECW world champion. Not surprisingly, Brunk changed his name to something a little more exotic—Sabu.

3. **MONTE SOPP**

As a member of The Smoking Gunns, Monte Sopp was a WWF tag-team champion in the mid-1990s. Wisely choosing not to call himself "Bad Ass" Monte Sopp, he changed his name to Billy Gunn.

4. **JAMES REIHEL**

James Reihel revolutionized the sport of professional wrestling with his high-flying maneuvers. In 1992, he was the first ECW world champion. By now you've probably guessed that James Reihel is Superfly Jimmy Snuka.

5. **LARRY PFOHL**

When Larry Pfohl began wrestling, he seemed to have it all—incredible strength and an amazing physique. He was good enough to win the WCW world title in 1991 and regained it in 1997. Pfohl became "The Total Package" only when he changed his name to Lex Luger.

6. **RODERICK TOOMBS**

Roderick Toombs sounds like a good real name for The Undertaker, but it's not. The former Toombs has been an intercontinental and United States champion and a force in wrestling for nearly thirty years. You may have heard of him. His name is Roddy Piper.

7. **ROBERT SZATOWSKI**

Robert Szatowski is probably the most talented wrestler in Extreme Championship Wrestling. He held the ECW television title for two years. He may refer to himself as "The Whole F****** Show," but he's better known as Rob Van Dam.

8. **ED FARHAT**

One of the most sadistic wrestlers in history, Ed Farhat was a perennial United States champion during the 1960s and 1970s. Known as "The Maniac of the Mat," he threw fire into the faces of wrestlers and bloodied their foreheads with foreign objects during his reign of terror. Few could have guessed that The Sheik's real name was Ed Farhat.

9. **JIM HELLWIG**

Jim Hellwig began his career as The Rock in the 1980s, though another wrestler gained greater fame with the name in the 1990s. Hellwig's early success came as The Dingo Warrior. By the time he won the WWF world title from Hulk Hogan in 1990, Hellwig was famous as The Ultimate Warrior. He later legally changed his name to Warrior Jim Hellwig.

10. **PAGE FALKINBURG**

Sometimes an aging wrestler will become a manager, but Page Falkinburg made the rare transition from manager to wrestler. His slow climb to the top was complete when, as Diamond Dallas Page, he won the WCW world heavyweight title in April 1999.

Incredible names

It's tough getting noticed in a sport as competitive as professional wrestling. Most young wrestlers need a gimmick to stand out from the crowd. The following wrestlers have selected names that would stand out in any phone book.

1. JUSTIN CREDIBLE

To become a wrestling star, the former P.J. Walker needed an incredible name. He called his finishing move, a spinning tombstone pile driver, That's Incredible. When he won the ECW world title in 2000, it was an achievement befitting a wrestler named Justin Credible.

2. STAMP LICKAGE

Anyone who watches the news knows that disgruntled postal employees can be dangerous. Stamp Lickage, a wrestling postman, is delivering pain to his opponents throughout the Midwest.

Amish Roadkill

Dr. Mike Lano

Amish Roadkill looks big enough to raise a barn all by himself. Despite his size, he is very skilled on the ropes.

3. **AMISH ROADKILL**

The Amish are known for their simple, peaceful lifestyle, but apparently no one ever told the wrestler Amish Roadkill. The 300-pound bearded grappler known as "The Angry Amish Chickenplucker" is a hardcore specialist. Amazingly agile, he can walk on the top rope and delivers a devastating splash.

4. **BRIMSTONE SHOCKER**

A former Hardcore Wrestling Alliance champion, Brimstone Shocker paired with Wild Child to form a tag team called The Screaming Demons. He has also teamed with The Coroner. Living up to his name, he sometimes shocks opponents with a cattle prod.

5. **DANCES WITH DUDLEY**

Yet another of the Dudley half-brothers, Dances with Dudley is supposedly the child of Daddy Dudley and a Sioux Indian.

6. **SMOKY MOUNTAIN MASSACRE**

Smoky Mountain Massacre made a name for himself in the 1990s while wrestling In the mid-South independent circuit. The 450-pounder is a former tag-team partner of Jesse James.

7. **SILKY BOOM BOOM**

During the late 1990s, the flamboyant Silky Boom Boom won a number of titles in the South despite weighing barely 200 pounds. He was half of the tag team known as Hot n' Heavy with 440-pound partner Frenchy Riviera.

8. CHAM PAIN

A native of Las Vegas, Cham Pain enjoys the good life. The former exotic dancer has held a number of regional championships. His finishing move is a reverse DDT, which he calls The Corkscrew.

9. TERRA RIZING

Hunter Hearst Helmsley's wrestling name when he began his career in 1992 was Terra Rizing. Under that name, he terrorized opponents throughout New England.

10. T. RANTULA

Wrestling's Spider-Man, T. Rantula wore tights with a spiderweb design. Managed by The Black Widow, the bearded big man won several regional championship belts in the late 1990s.

notable nicknames

Many wrestlers are better known for their nicknames than for their ring names. Here are some of wrestling's most distinctive nicknames.

1. **THE DOGFACED GREMLIN**

Rick Steiner and his brother Scott won WCW tag-team titles six times between 1991 and 1998. Rick, referred to as "The Dogfaced Gremlin," later feuded with his brother, now called "Big Poppa Pump." After the breakup of the Steiner Brothers, Rick teamed with Kenny Khaos to win the tag title.

2. **THE AMERICAN DREAM**

Dusty Rhodes first won the National Wrestling Alliance world title from Harley Race in 1979. The champion of the common man, Rhodes was known as The American Dream.

3. **THE ALBINO RHINO**

Danger, the former World of Hurt champion, had two nicknames: The Albino Rhino and The One-Ton Human Wrecking Machine. His finishing move was called The Danger Zone.

4. THE MOUTH OF THE SOUTH

Jimmy Hart has been one of wrestling's premier managers for more than twenty years. He intentionally irritates and distracts his wrestlers' opponents and the referees by incessantly talking, usually through a megaphone. His constant chatter has earned him his nickname, The Mouth of the South.

5. THE NINTH WONDER OF THE WORLD

There were seven wonders of the ancient world. Andre the Giant was dubbed The Eighth Wonder of the World. Wrestling's wonder woman, Chyna, has earned her nickname as The Ninth Wonder of the World by defeating male wrestlers with regularity.

6. THE MACHO MAN

A wrestling superstar for more than a decade, Randy Savage is one of the few wrestlers ever to win both the WWF and WCW world titles. Savage was given the nickname the Macho Man because of his insensitive treatment of his valet/manager Elizabeth, who also happened to be his wife. Early in his career, he would make her remove his robe and hold the ropes for him. If anything went wrong, he would berate her.

7. STRANGLER

Ed "Strangler" Lewis is considered one of the greatest wrestlers of all time. Lewis won the National Wrestling Alliance world championship five times between 1920 and 1932. He got the nickname "Strangler" because of his devastating side headlock that was thought by some to be a stranglehold.

8. **THE TOAST OF THE EAST COAST**

Dr. Jerry Graham was one of the famed wrestling Graham Brothers. A major star in the 1950s and 1960s, Graham proclaimed himself "The Toast of the East Coast." Blond and overweight, he rivaled Gorgeous George as the man wrestling fans most loved to hate. He excelled as a tag-team wrestler and won many titles with his brothers.

9. **THE NATURE BOY**

"Nature Boy" is such a good nickname that two of the sport's greatest champions used it. "Nature Boy" Buddy Rogers won both the NWA and WWF world titles in the late 1950s and early 1960s. "Nature Boy" Ric Flair has also held world titles in both major federations. At last count Flair had been world champion seventeen times. Even though he's over fifty, he still goes by the name of Nature Boy.

10. **THE BODY**

During his wrestling days, Jesse Ventura was nicknamed "The Body" because he bragged that he had the best physique in professional wrestling. During his successful campaign for the governorship of Minnesota in 1998, Ventura changed his nickname to "The Mind."

One Word Says It All

You know someone has made it big in show business when he's instantly recognizable by a one-word name. When it was announced that Elvis left the building, no one asked, "Elvis who?" Wrestling superstars such as Sting, Kane, Goldberg, Mankind, and Tazz are known by one-word names. Here are some other wrestlers with one-of-a-kind names.

1. **CREMATOR**

Cremator is a masked 300-pound wrestler who in many ways resembles The Undertaker. Like The Undertaker, he sits up after seemingly being knocked out, and he has a dark side to his character. Cremator likes to compete in burial matches and claims he hails from "man's deepest fears."

2. **EDGE**

Not to be confused with the guitarist from the rock group U2, Edge has gone through metamorphoses during his stay in the WWF. He was a member of The Brood and a follower in The Undertaker's Ministry of Darkness. In July 1999, he briefly held the intercontinental title after defeating Jeff Jarrett.

3. **MEAT**

The son of former WWF world champion Stan "The Man" Stasiak, Shawn Stasiak briefly wrestled under the name "Meat." Since joining WCW, Stasiak goes by the name "Perfection."

4. **PSICOSIS**

Acrobatic Mexican star Psicosis is one of wrestling's great innovators. His unpredictability has resulted in many memorable matches, most notably with Rey Misterio Jr. and La Parka. One of his most effective finishing moves is the guillotine leg-drop.

5. **TEST**

Test seemed to have an inside track to stardom when it was announced that he was engaged to Stephanie McMahon, daughter of WWF owner Vince McMahon. The union fell through when Stephanie "married" Hunter Hearst Helmsley. Recently, Test has competed in the tag team T & A with partner Prince Albert.

6. **HATER**

One of the most hated wrestlers in the Midwest independent federations, Hater lives up to his name by his disrespect for opponents and fans. Previously, he wrestled under the name of The Punisher.

7. **ATLANTIS**

The continent of Atlantis is still lost, but you can usually find Atlantis wrestling in Mexico. The veteran has held a number of middleweight and light-heavyweight titles south of the border.

8. **RATBOY**

The National Wrestling Council champion in the late 1990s, Ratboy has wrestled mainly on the East Coast. His finishing move is The Cat Trap.

9. **MENG**

For more than two decades, Meng has been one of wrestling's most feared competitors. He and The Barbarian formed one of the dominant tag teams in wrestling history. The merciless one's submission hold is the dreaded Tongan Death Grip.

10. **HUMONGOUS**

A star in Texas, this 400-pounder was a member of Generation X-Treme. Opponents don't get up after his Humongous Drop.

They're Animals

M any wrestlers could be described as animals in the ring, and some even use animal names. Over the years wrestlers have been called everything from moose to piranah.

1. JAKE "THE SNAKE" ROBERTS

Jake Roberts is not only nicknamed "The Snake," he brings one to the ring. The snake is usually a huge python named Damian, but occasionally Jake has pulled a cobra out of his bag. The deadly snake once bit Randy Savage. When Jake defeated an opponent, often with his DDT move, he draped the python over his victim.

2. GORILLA MONSOON

Born in New York, Gino Marella wrestled under the more fearsome name of Gorilla Monsoon and supposedly hailed from the far reaches of Manchuria. At more than 400 pounds, Monsoon was a top contender in the WWF for many years before becoming one of wrestling's most respected commentators.

3. **THE JUNKYARD DOG**

Sylvester Ritter, better known as The Junkyard Dog, wore a dog chain around his neck and numerous belts, including the North American heavyweight title, around his waist. J.Y.D. frequently used his hard head to weaken opponents and then finished them off with his power slam, The Big Thump. The popular wrestler died in an automobile accident in 1998.

4. **BOBBY "THE WEASEL" HEENAN**

Bobby Heenan would rather be called "The Brain," but during his days as a manager of many of the sport's biggest heels, he was known to the fans as "The Weasel." Whenever he was at ringside, fans would irritate him by chanting this nickname.

5. **RHINO**

A rising star in Extreme Championship Wrestling, Rhino's brawling style makes him a natural in a federation notorious for its no-holds-barred matches. One of his most effective moves is to charge across the ring and gore his opponent in the midsection.

6. **MOONDOG SPOT**

The Moondogs were the WWF tag-team champions in 1981. Moondog Spot exhibited many canine qualities, including eating raw meat and howling. His best move was to hit an opponent over the head with a bone.

7. WOODY WOODCHUCK

While he may not have the sport's most intimidating name, Woody Woodchuck has held numerous title belts in the South during the 1990s. Woodchuck dresses in the outfit of a backwoodsman.

8. THE ITALIAN STALLION

A former star in the WCW, The Italian Stallion held numerous regional championship belts in the 1990s. His claim to fame is that he is the world record-holder for spaghetti eating.

9. RICKY "THE DRAGON" STEAMBOAT

The dragon may be an imaginary animal, but the success of Ricky "The Dragon" Steamboat was quite real. The popular Hawaiian was one of the dominant wrestlers of the 1980s. He won the intercontinental title in 1987 and the WCW heavyweight belt in 1989.

10. BLUE PANTHER

Panthers in the wild are black, but wrestling's Blue Panther is a cat of a different color. The Mexican star has won numerous middleweight titles. A master of submission holds, his favorite is the standing figure-four deathlock.

Beasts, Bruisers, and Brutes

Professional wrestling can be a brutal sport. The men featured in this list were some of wrestling's roughest competitors.

1. DICK THE BRUISER

Before he became a professional wrestler, Dick Afflis played four seasons as an offensive lineman with the Green Bay Packers. As Dick the Bruiser, he lived up to his reputation as "The World's Most Dangerous Wrestler." Five times he and The Crusher won world tag-team titles. The pinnacle of his career came in 1966 when he defeated Mad Dog Vachon for the AWA world title.

2. THE CRUSHER

Reggie "The Crusher" Lisowski claimed he trained by dancing the polka and running laps with kegs of beer on his shoulders. It must have worked, because the powerhouse from Milwaukee won the AWA world heavyweight title three times between 1963 and 1965 and was the AWA tag-team titlist with five different partners: Dick the Bruiser,

Verne Gagne, Billy Robinson, Baron Von Raschke, and Red Bastien.

3. **BRUISER BRODY**

At six feet, eight inches tall and 320 pounds, Bruiser Brody was one of wrestling's toughest and wildest men. He often rendered opponents senseless with kicks from his animal-skin boots.

4. **BRUTE BERNARD**

Wrestling fans of the sixties will no doubt remember the bald bruiser known as Brute Bernard. The Brute beat opponents to a pulp. His finishing move was called The Pulverizer. The Brute teamed with Skull Murphy to win the United States tag-team title in 1963.

5. **THE BEAST FROM THE EAST**

The 370-pound "Beast from the East," Bam Bam Bigelow has been a top contender in the WWF, WCW, and ECW. His top-rope moonsault has defeated many an opponent. Despite all his success, he is best remembered for his loss to football star Lawrence Taylor at Wrestlemania XI.

6. **CRUSHER VERDU**

Oscar "Crusher" Verdu was one of the few wrestlers ever to defeat the great Bruno Sammartino. Wrestling primarily on the West Coast, he was managed at different times by Captain Lou Albano and Roddy Piper. In 1976, he teamed with Piper to win the NWA America's tag-team title.

7. **THE BEAST**

Dan "The Beast" Severn is a former Ultimate Fighting champion. He had a bitter rivalry with another Ultimate Fighting champion, Ken Shamrock. The Beast used his array of submission holds to defend his NWA title for four years.

8. **BRUISER MASTINO**

Weighing in at more than 400 pounds, Bruiser Mastino has been a top draw on the East Coast. He had a brief stint in the WWF as The Mantaur, half man, half beast.

9. **BRUISER BEDLAM**

Bruiser Bedlam is a brawler who has had memorable feuds with Mick Foley and Al Snow. Managed by Handsome Johnny Bradford, he wrestled on the Midwest circuit in the late 1990s.

10. **THE BRUISE BROTHERS**

Twin brothers Ron and Don Harris wrestled for a time as The Bruise Brothers. During their tenure in the WWF, they were known as The Grimm Twins.

Crazy for You

Not all wrestlers are playing with a full deck. The only people crazier than the following wrestlers are the opponents who stepped into the ring with them.

1. MORGUS THE MANIAC

Supposedly a mental patient from the Bellevue State Hospital, Morgus the Maniac arrives at the ring in a straight jacket. Accompanied by a doctor and a nurse, he is uncontrollable once the match starts. The Maniac is most often seen in Maryland and Virginia.

2. THE MACEDONIAN MADMAN

"The Macedonian Madman," Chris Markoff, won many titles around the world in the 1960s and 1970s. The rule-breaker also held several regional belts including the California and Florida state titles. He once boasted that he had buried more men than any undertaker ever could. He teamed with Angelo Poffo to form the tag team The Devil's Duo.

3. CRAZY LUKE GRAHAM

The craziest member of the Graham clan, Luke Graham said that the only reason there was a rule book was so that he could violate it. His idea of having a good time was to hurt people. Graham and partner Tarzan Tyler were the WWF tag-team champions in 1971. Graham's favorite illegal move was to jab his taped fist into his opponent's throat. When the fans chanted "Crazy Luke," he went totally berserk.

4. MAD DOG VACHON

Maurice "Mad Dog" Vachon won the American Wrestling Alliance world heavyweight title in 1964. A wildman in and out of the ring, he delighted in raking his razor-sharp fingernails down an opponent's back. Former AWA world champion Nick Bockwinkel said that Mad Dog Vachon was the most vicious wrestler of all time, and few would disagree.

5. MADMAN PONDO

Arguably the wildest wrestler of the last decade, Madman Pondo will use anything he can get his hands on—a stop sign, garbage-can lid, or a barbed-wire baseball bat—to batter his opponents into submission. He once wrestled in a ring filled with cacti and pools of rubbing alcohol, which he rubbed into the open wounds of his opponent.

6. THE BERZERKER

If you never saw The Berzerker wrestle, then imagine Bruiser Brody in a Viking outfit. The Icelandic warrior came to the ring wearing a horned helmet and carrying a sword and shield. Managed by Mr. Fuji, the 320-pound Viking pillaged the WWF in the early 1990s.

7. MADD MAXXINE

People thought she was crazy when she began wrestling men, but Madd Maxxine defeated males with regularity and even held regional championship belts. The 200-pound Maxxine wears face paint, not makeup, which makes her look even more demented.

8. HORACE THE PSYCHOPATH

Supposedly a former patient at St. Peter's Mental Hospital, Horace the Psychopath is a favorite in Minnesota, a state with a special fondness for wrestlers. Horace shows little regard for his own safety in the ring and even less for his opponents.

9. SUPER CRAZY

Super Crazy was a star in Mexico before becoming widely known to American audiences in Extreme Championship Wrestling. Renowned for his high-flying skills, he has also wrestled under the names of Super Loco and Hysteria.

10. MANIAC MARK LEWIN

Mark Lewin had a schizophrenic career during his heyday in the 1960s and 1970s. Sometimes he assumed the role of the handsome good guy, facing such despised opponents as The Sheik. As Maniac Mark Lewin, he was a crazed, twitching madman who enjoyed maiming other wrestlers. Lewin teamed with Don Curtis to win the WWF tag-team title in 1958.

Deadly Intent

In recent years, the death match has come into vogue, but wrestlers have been calling themselves "killers" since the sport's inception. Here is a most-wanted list of wrestling's ten deadliest competitors.

1. KILLER KOWALSKI

The original Killer, Wladek Kowalski was one of the most hated wrestlers of the 1950s. Tall, lean, and mean, Kowalski bit, kicked, and gouged his way to wrestling immortality. His most feared move was his throat stomp, in which he leaped off the top rope onto an opponent's neck. One night in Montreal in 1954, Kowalski performed the move against Yukon Eric. The Killer's aim was slightly off, and he landed on Yukon Eric's cauliflower ear, tearing it off. Bruno Sammartino remarked that Killer Kowalski was the most vicious man he ever faced in the ring.

2. KILLER TIM BROOKS

Bobo Brazil once said of Tim Brooks, "He's going to kill someone someday." If Killer Brooks didn't succeed in putting a man six feet under, it wasn't for lack of trying. The bearded man with the skull and crossbones on his trunks boasted he was the sport's only killer. "I've got a mean streak from the back of my neck to the tip of my toes," he warned. Brooks's most dangerous weapon was a loaded elbow, which he used to crack skulls.

3. DR. DEATH STEVE WILLIAMS

Dr. Death Steve Williams was a college football star at the University of Oklahoma prior to becoming a professional wrestler. His rough, tough image has made him a popular attraction in both the United States and Japan. Williams employs a number of devastating put-away moves, most notably The Doctor Bomb, Backdrop Driver, and his signature, The Oklahoma Stampede.

4. KILLER KHAN

Killer Khan will always be remembered as the man who broke Andre the Giant's leg. It was thought that Andre was indestructible until the Mongolian giant jumped off the top rope and broke Andre's leg in two places.

5. THE LETHAL WEAPON

Martial-arts expert Steve Blackman proudly answers to his nickname, The Lethal Weapon. Besides unleashing a deadly arsenal of kicks, Blackman occasionally uses a kendo stick to soften up an opponent for the kill. The Lethal Weapon's favorite execution move is appropriately called The Guillotine.

6. BUDDY "KILLER" AUSTIN

Buddy "Killer" Austin teamed with The Great Scott to win the WWF tag-team title in March 1963. Austin usually finished off his opponent with The Indian Deathlock.

7. KILLER KARL KOX

A notorious rule-breaker of the 1970s, Killer Karl Kox formed a lethal tag team with Killer Karl Krupp. His brainbuster was one of the most devastating holds in professional wrestling. Kox also was known as "The Crippler."

8. NATURAL BORN KILLERS

The Natural Born Killers were a 1990s tag team composed of Glen Osbourne and The Rockin' Rebel. Osbourne, known as "The Bad Man from the Badlands," was also a tag-team champion with partner Flash Flanagan.

9. THE CAREER KILLER

Former Extreme Championship Wrestling champion Mike Awesome was called "The Career Killer" because of the number of wrestlers he injured. In 2000, while wrestling in the WCW, Awesome temporarily paralyzed Kanyon at the pay-per-view Slamboree.

10. KILLER SAM SHEPPARD

Dr. Sam Sheppard was a Cleveland physician convicted of murdering his wife in 1954. More than a decade later, he was released from prison after being found not guilty at a retrial. He became a professional wrestler and was billed as "Killer" Sam Sheppard, a nickname he hated. He married the daughter of a wrestling promoter. His finishing move was The Mandible Claw, a hold made famous thirty years later by Mankind.

Call Me Mister T

M r. T is not the only Mister to participate in professional wrestling. If you address any of the following wrestlers, you better call them "Mister."

1. **MR. PERFECT**

Curt Hennig defeated Nick Bockwinkel to win the AWA world title in 1987. When he joined the WWF, he became Mr. Perfect. According to Hennig, everything he did was perfect. His wrestling may not have been perfect, but it was good enough to win him the intercontinental title in 1990.

2. **MR. WONDERFUL**

Paul Orndorff was one of the WWF's biggest stars in the mid-1980s. He and Roddy Piper faced Hulk Hogan and Mr. T in the main event of the first Wrestlemania. Known as Mr. Wonderful, Orndorff had "Mr. #1derful" written on his trunks.

3. MR. FUJI

The devious Mr. Fuji won the WWF tag-team title three times with Professor Toro Tanaka in the 1970s and twice more with Master Saito in the 1980s. His subsequent career as a manager was just as successful. Fuji liked to hit opponents with his cane when the referee wasn't looking.

4. MISTER M

Dr. Bill Miller was one of wrestling's premier stars forty years ago. Wearing a mask, he wrestled under the name of Mister M. In 1962, Mister M captured the AWA world championship.

5. MR. HUGHES

At six feet, five inches tall and 310 pounds, Mr. Hughes has been an enforcer in numerous federations around the country. The big man's wrestling attire includes a white shirt, tie, suspenders, and sunglasses. Hughes formed a powerful tag team with Vader.

6. MR. ELECTRICITY

Not to be confused with the British grappler Lord Steven Regal, Steve Regal was a star of the 1980s who was nicknamed Mr. Electricity. Regal teamed with Gorgeous Jimmy Garvin to win the AWA tag-team title in 1985.

7. MR. OOH LA LA

This Frenchman is best known for his pre-match striptease, which he can never seem to accomplish without losing his balance. An outstanding tag-team wrestler, he combined with the wrestling chef, D.Z. Gillespie, to win regional tag belts.

8. **MR. EXCELLENT**

He may not be Mr. Perfect, but at least he's Mr. Excellent. Like Mr. Perfect, Mr. Excellent uses a powerplex as his finishing move. The martial-arts expert made his name in the late 1990s in Atlantic Coast promotions.

9. **MR. NIEBLA**

Like most wrestlers under 200 pounds, Mr. Niebla is a master of aerial moves. This masked man prefers a standing figure-four leg lock, The Nieblina, as his submission move.

10. **MISTER PAY-PER-VIEW**

Rob Van Dam has dominated his foes in Extreme Championship Wrestling for the last several years. He has been so unbeatable on ECW marquee events that he has earned the nickname Mister Pay-Per-View.

Keeping the Day Job

What do professional wrestlers do for a living? Some would have you believe that they have other professions outside the ring.

1. IRWIN R. SCHYSTER

Mike Rotundo, a very successful wrestler in the 1980s, assumed the role of IRS agent Irwin R. Schyster in the WWF during the early 1990s. IRS entered the ring wearing red suspenders, a white shirt, tie, and black pants. He carried a briefcase which he said contained proof that his opponents were tax cheats, and he threatened to audit them. His finishing move was a fall-away body slam called The Write-Off.

2. D.Z. GILLESPIE

D.Z. Gillespie wore a white chef's hat and outfit into the ring. The 400-pound chef hated to lose a cooking or eating contest almost as much as he hated to lose a wrestling match.

Gillespie often used his reliable cookie sheet as a weapon, although his finisher was The Bunseye Splash.

3. REPO MAN

When he wasn't repossessing cars, Repo Man was wreaking havoc in the World Wrestling Federation in the early 1990s. Wearing a blindfold mask, Repo Man used every sneaky move to win a match. The Crowbar was his finisher. He often tied his opponents' ankles with a towline.

4. PROF. EGON ECTON

Hailing from Three Mile Island, Egon Ecton claimed to be a science professor. He wrestled in a lab coat and sometimes dyed his hair different colors. One of his more memorable tag-team partners was named The Lab Experiment.

5. ISAAC YANKEM

Before he was Kane, The Big Red Machine, Glenn Jacobs was wrestling's evil dentist, Isaac Yankem. Judging from his crooked, rotten teeth, Yankem needed a dentist himself.

6. DR. HURTZ

Dr. Hurtz made house calls along the East Coast in the 1990s. Managed by Nurse Fifi, the good doctor finished off his opponents with The Flatliner or a splash from the top rope known as The DOA.

7. BULL BULLINSKI

Bull Bullinski, the wrestling truck driver, was a star in the

American Wrestling Alliance during the 1970s. Bullinski once defeated Bobby Heenan in a truck driver's death match in which they both wore brass knuckles.

8. BRUTUS "THE BARBER" BEEFCAKE

Brutus Beefcake earned the name "The Barber" because of his propensity for cutting his opponents' hair. The Barber brought a pair of shears into the ring and celebrated victories by giving the loser a trim. Beefcake cut Adrian Adonis's locks at Wrestlemania III and silenced "The Mouth of the South" Jimmy Hart by cutting his hair at Wrestlemania IV.

9. CHIP FAIRWAY

Chip Fairway is professional wrestling's most avid golfer. Fairway and his valet, a Big Bertha driver, have headlined on the Midwest circuit. Even his two best finishing moves, The Sandtrap and The Titanium Driver, are golf-related.

10. MAD ANTHONY MCMURPHY

Mad Anthony McMurphy is professional wrestling's cab driver. McMurphy has been picking up fares in the Heartland Wrestling Association.

Gorgeous Georges

Gorgeous George was one of the first wrestlers fans loved to hate. Although he was anything but gorgeous, George Wagner annoyed fans with his vanity. Here are some of wrestling's self-proclaimed pretty boys.

1. RAVISHING RICK RUDE

Ravishing Rick Rude was always his own biggest fan. He would remind you how ravishing he was at every opportunity. "Simply Ravishing" was written on his robe, and he had a woman's face painted on the back of his tights. Before a match, Rude would wiggle his butt in a provocative manner. Women fainted when he kissed them. Rude held many title belts over the years, including the intercontinental title in 1989 and the United States heavyweight belt in 1991.

2. GORGEOUS JIMMY GARVIN

With his dark curly hair, mustache, and beard, Jimmy Garvin was proof that beauty was in the eye of the beholder. Gorgeous Jimmy owned a wardrobe as flamboyant as his personality. He usually entered the ring dressed in rhinestone tights, with a feather boa draped over his neck. He was accompanied by his valet, Precious. In 1985, Garvin combined with Steve Regal to win the AWA world tag-team title.

3. HANDSOME JOHNNY BAREND

An accomplished tag-team wrestler, Handsome Johnny Barend paired with The Frenchman, Magnificent Maurice, to win many regional titles. In July 1962, he teamed with Nature Boy Buddy Rogers to capture the WWF world tag-team title.

4. "THE MODEL" RICK MARTEL

Rick Martel won the American Wrestling Alliance world title in 1984. A fan favorite for much of his career, he teamed with both Tony Garea and Tito Santana to win WWF tag-team titles. In the early 1990s, he returned to the World Wrestling Foundation as "The Model" Rick Martel. He boasted that he was the best-dressed man in the world. Martel developed his own cologne, which he called Arrogance. He would spray it around the ring before matches and sometimes blinded his opponents by spraying it in their eyes.

5. HANDSOME JIMMY VALIANT

One of pro wrestling's most rugged stars of the 1970s and 1980s, Handsome Jimmy Valiant wore a long white beard, which made him look like a member of the rock band ZZ Top. Valiant was also known as The Boogie Woogie Man. He formed a respected tag team with his brother, Luscious Johnny Valiant.

6. JOHNNY HANDSOME

Known as "Mr. Infatuation," Johnny Handsome has won several titles in the Northeast. The arrogant wrestler calls himself the most handsome man in the sport. He often wears a bow tie.

7. HANDSOME FRANK STALLETTO

Frank Stalletto is another wrestler who claims to be the sport's most handsome. Handsome Frank has done most of his wrestling in the East. His finishing move is called The Handsome Driver.

8. BEAUTIFUL BOBBY EATON

Beautiful Bobby Eaton teamed with Pretty Boy Stan Lane to win the NWA world tag-team title in 1988. Four years later, Beautiful Bobby paired with Arn Anderson to win the world tag-team title a second time.

9. BEAUTIFUL BOBBY REMUS

Anyone who has seen Sgt. Slaughter wrestle may find it hard to believe that he began as a pretty boy. One of his first wrestling personas was Beautiful Bobby Remus.

10. HANDSOME JOHNNY VALENTINE

The father of champion wrestler Greg Valentine, Handsome Johnny Valentine was the original "Blonde Bomber." A star of the 1960s, the methodical wrestler frequently finished off his opponents with a move he called The Atomic Skullcrusher.

Not Just Another Pretty Face

For every pretty-boy wrestler, you'll find another who's dog ugly, but even a dog would howl at these ten men.

1. THE FRENCH ANGEL

Maurice Tillet, The French Angel, suffered from a glandular disorder that disfigured his features. This 1950s wrestler was so hideous that he was billed as a monstrosity.

2. BUSHWACKER LUKE

Luke Williams, a member of The Bushwackers tag team, may have won many wrestling titles during his career, but he certainly never won any beauty contests. With no front teeth and a heavily scarred forehead, he looked like a creation from the mind of Goya. His tag-team partner, Butch Miller, was no charmer either.

3. WILD BULL CURRY

Beetle-browed Bull Curry was so ugly that he actually traumatized spectators. Wrestling in his hometown of Hartford,

Connecticut, he once began pummeling an opponent out-side the ring. A little girl at ringside was so frightened by Curry that she began to scream and had to be carried from the arena by her father. "His face scared me," she said.

4. GEORGE "THE ANIMAL" STEELE

A cinch on anyone's short list of ugly wrestlers, George "The Animal" Steele has been described as looking like a Neanderthal. With his ridged bald head, hairy back, and green tongue, Steele was truly an animal.

5. ERIC THE RED

Eric the Red wore a helmet with horns and dressed in a Viking outfit. He often clubbed opponents with a giant bone he carried to the ring. Also known as Eric the Animal, he looked as though he hadn't washed his hair since the era of the original Vikings.

6. ISAAC YANKEM

Glenn Jacobs has had two hideously ugly personas—Isaac Yankem, the demented dentist, had crooked, yellow teeth; Kane, who wore a mask, had been badly burned in a fire. When the McMahons removed Kane's mask, they cringed at the sight of his face.

7. DUSTY RHODES

Dusty Rhodes was a great wrestler and had the body of an Adonis—Adrian Adonis. Clearly, The American Dream was no dreamboat. Rhodes' forehead showed the marks of many mat battles, and he had dark rings around his eyes. He was grossly overweight, heavily scarred, and had a patch of discolored skin on his right side.

8. BARON VON RASCHKE

Bald, with misshapen ears and an unsettling grimace, Baron Von Raschke has never been mistaken for The Heartbreak Kid. He was so ugly that he frightened small children.

9. JOE LE DUC

The Canadian Lumberjack Joe Le Duc always had an insane look on his face. His matches were often bloodbaths, and Le Duc's face was often masked with crimson.

10. THE CUBAN ASSASSINS

The Cuban Assassins were a tag team in the 1970s. Bearded like their hero, Fidel Castro, they looked like Cheech and Chong on a bad trip.

Too Sexy for Their Trunks

M any wrestlers claim to have superhuman sex appeal. Kevin Nash is known to his female fans as "Big Sexy." Brian Christopher had "Too Sexy" inscribed on his trunks. Jimmy "The Gigolo" Del Ray wrestled in a tag team called The Heavenly Bodies. Stylin' Shane Eden refers to himself as "Wrestling's Sexiest Thing."

1.   VAL VENIS

Val Venis claimed he was an adult film star before he turned to wrestling. Prior to matches, Venis showed films of himself in bed with attractive females. His finishing move, a splash off the top rope, is named The Money Shot. Venis won the intercontinental title in 1998 and the European championship belt in 1999. Oddly, the one title he has not won in the World Wrestling Federation is the hardcore championship.

2.   BRAD ARMSTRONG

The son of wrestler Bob Armstrong, Brad was the NWA rookie of the year in 1982 and won the National heavyweight title the following year. Armstrong has appeared in adult films, including a hardcore wrestling movie called *Headlock*.

3. **THE GODFATHER**

Professional wrestling's resident pimp, The Godfather, was escorted to the ring by several scantily clad ladies known as his "hos." He invited the crowd to "hop aboard my ho train."

4. **SEXUAL CHOCOLATE**

Mark Henry was an Olympic-caliber weightlifter before becoming a professional wrestler. Billed as "The World's Strongest Man," the 400-pound Henry became an unlikely sex object. Henry was known as "Sexual Chocolate" and, according to the story line, impregnated a 79-year-old wrestler, Mae Young. In August 1999, Henry won the WWF European title.

5. **SHAWN MICHAELS**

Shawn Michaels prided himself for his reputation as "The Heartbreak Kid." On his left arm is a tattoo of a heart with a knife through it. The "Boy Toy" once posed for a *Playgirl* pictorial. After a successful career as a tag-team wrestler, Michaels won the WWF world heavyweight title three times between 1996 and 1997.

6. **LADIES' CHOICE**

A rising star in the Pacific Northwest, Ladies' Choice is accompanied by his valet, Veronika Lake. He finishes off his opponents with a frog splash which he calls The Night Stand.

7. **JUSTIN ST. JOHN**

Justin St. John claimed to be the sexiest man on the planet. When he wasn't being sexy, St. John was also the North American All-Star Wrestling champion in the mid-1990s.

8. AUSTIN IDOL

Blonde, tanned, and muscular, Austin Idol was known as "The Universal Heartbreak" in the 1980s. He claimed that hundreds of women swooned over him. Idol strutted his way to numerous wrestling titles in the Southeast.

9. PLAYBOY BUDDY ROSE

Despite weighing nearly 300 pounds and possessing a less than Adonis-like body, Buddy Rose boasted of a playboy lifestyle. He explained that he neglected his physique in order to relax at his mansion while being attended by beautiful women. The Playboy teamed with Pretty Boy Doug Somers to win the AWA world tag-team title in 1986.

10. FRENCHY RIVIERA

Another unlikely sex symbol, the 440-pound Frenchy Riviera claims to be a stripper from the French Riviera. Also known as Keith Arden, he was a member of The Centerfolds tag team.

Ric Flair

Nature Boy Ric Flair's flamboyant style and long list of WWF and WCW titles made him the "Cadillac of Champions."

Clothes Make the Wrestler

In the old days of professional wrestling, almost all the wrestlers wore tights in the ring. When Gorgeous George began wearing frilly robes, other wrestlers realized that their outfits were an important part of establishing their personas. The following wrestlers dressed for success.

1. RIC FLAIR

Nature Boy Ric Flair earned his nickname as "The Cadillac of Champions" by wearing some of the most fabulous robes ever seen in the wrestling ring. Slick Ric paid thousands of dollars for the glittering robes, which became his trademark. "Styling and profiling," Flair has won the WWF and WCW titles a record seventeen times since 1981.

2. JESSE VENTURA

No wrestler ever wore more outrageous ring apparel than Jesse "The Body" Ventura. Ventura may wear conservative suits in his present position as the governor of Minnesota, but his wrestling outfits were always outlandish. A typical Ventura getup consisted of sunglasses, bandanas, feather boas, and tie-dyed tights.

3. **FRED BLASSIE**

Late in his wrestling career, Fred Blassie became a popular favorite on the West Coast. He was known as "The Hollywood Fashion Plate" for his spectacular robes and colorful trunks. After his wrestling career, Blassie maintained his fashion-plate image as a manager.

4. **RANDY SAVAGE**

The Macho Man Randy Savage is one of the few men to win the world title in both the World Wrestling Federation and World Championship Wrestling. Savage was one of the first wrestlers to wear colorful bodysuits. He also accessorized his wardrobe with outrageous sunglasses and hats.

5. **SLICKY BOY**

One of the most style-conscious wrestlers, Slicky Boy dresses in a tuxedo. Always wanting to look his best, he frequently combs his hair during a match and even uses the comb to attack his opponent.

6. **EL MATADOR**

Tito Santana won the intercontinental title in 1984. In the early 1990s, the native of Tocula, Mexico, wrestled under the name of El Matador. Santana entered the ring in the matador's traditional "suit of lights."

7. **THE HEADBANGERS**

The Headbangers, Mosh and Thrasher, held the WWF tag-team title in 1997. During their matches, they wear kilts, although their opponents frequently accuse them of wearing dresses.

8. **MASTER MAYHEM**

Nearly seven feet tall and over 300 pounds, Master Mayhem is an imposing figure in the ring. His slick leather outfit and mask make him even more intimidating. The master of mayhem has rarely been defeated and has held numerous championships in the South.

9. **PRETTY BOY STAN LANE**

One of the few wrestlers who could rival Nature Boy Ric Flair's wardrobe was Pretty Boy Stan Lane. He wore some of the most beautifully decorated robes ever seen in a wrestling ring. Lane teamed with Beautiful Bobby Eaton to win the NWA world tag-team title in 1988 and later paired with Eddie Golden in the tag team known as The Gorgeous Blondes.

10. **GORGEOUS GEORGE JUNIOR**

Gorgeous George set the standard for ornate ring attire. In the 1970s, his son, Gorgeous George Junior, carried on the family tradition. Accompanied by his valet, Frenchie, Junior's frilly pink robes were every bit as outlandish as those of his famous father.

Totally Outrageous

Professional wrestling has always pushed the envelope of outrageousness. No gimmick is too wild, and bad taste knows no limit in the ring.

1. DARREN DROZDOV

Darren Drozdov is remembered for many things, none of them normal. Droz pierced Val Venis' nose on a WWF broadcast and was the man who threw Hawk off the TitanTron. Drozdov liked to cross-dress in the ring and had a particular affinity for stockings. What set Droz apart from other wrestlers was his amazing ability to vomit on command. The disgusting habit earned him the nickname "Puke."

2. THE GARGOYLE

If anyone could give Droz a run for his money as wrestling's most disgusting performer of the late 1990s, it had to be the bald fiend known as The Gargoyle. One of his most bizarre moves was to sniff and lick his opponents' feet. He also enjoyed eating his own earwax.

3. **TRICKY RICKI STARR**

Tricky Ricki Starr shook up the macho world of professional wrestling when he rose to stardom in the 1950s. A trained dancer, Starr pranced into the ring in ballet slippers. Most opponents couldn't wait to get at him, but to everyone's surprise, Starr's acrobatic moves usually allowed him to defeat much larger and more powerful wrestlers. Tricky Ricki would perform pirouettes or slap his opponent and run across the ring. Incredibly, he became an action film star in Europe during the 1960s.

4. **DOINK THE CLOWN**

Another wrestling trickster was Doink the Clown. His identity concealed by clown makeup, Doink often confused opponents by having other wrestlers impersonate him—suddenly a wrestler was facing three or four Doinks. A midget clown named Dink also served as a distraction.

5. **GOLDUST**

Dustin Runnels, the son of wrestling legend Dusty Rhodes, made little impact in World Championship Wrestling, but when he debuted as Goldust in the World Wrestling Federation, people took notice. He dressed in a gold bodysuit, wore face paint, and covered his short blonde hair with a long blonde wig. He raised questions about his sexuality by trying to kiss Razor Ramon. On one occasion, he appeared in a huge diaper. Eventually, Runnels tired of Goldust and burned his costume.

6. **LEATHERFACE**

Inspired by a character in the cult horror film *The Texas Chainsaw Massacre,* Leatherface carried a chainsaw into the ring, often scattering fans along the way. He claimed that the mask was made from the faces of vanquished foes.

7. ADORABLE ADRIAN ADONIS

Adrian Adonis began his wrestling career as a leather-clad street tough from Hell's Kitchen. He teamed with Jesse "The Body" Ventura to form a tag team known as The East-West Connection. Adonis and Ventura won the AWA world tag-team belts in July 1980. Adonis and partner "Captain Redneck" Dick Murdoch captured the WWF tag-team title in April 1984. Fans were stunned when Adrian transformed himself into Adorable Adrian Adonis, an openly gay wrestler. Adonis, a married man in real life, hated the outrageous persona and died in an automobile accident in 1988 before he could re-establish his reputation as one of the sport's best wrestlers.

8. THE BLUE MEANIE

You can't help but notice The Blue Meanie. The 350-pounder had blue hair and wore painted-on glasses. He claimed to be from Pepperland, on a mission to take control of the universe. Remarkably agile for his size, he used a moonsault as his finishing move.

9. RANDY SAVAGE

At Wrestlemania IV, The Macho Man Randy Savage defeated Ted DiBiase to win the WWF championship. Readers of *The WWF Magazine* weren't surprised. The magazine, which came out two weeks before Wrestlemania, had referred to Savage as the WWF champion. WWF officials denied that the outcome was predetermined and claimed that the reference to Randy Savage as champion was a typographical error. Years before, *The Cincinnati Enquirer* had stopped carrying wrestling results in its sports page when the promoter called in the winners before the matches had occurred.

10. **BASTION BOOGER**

Bastion Booger has grossed out wrestling fans wherever he has appeared. His 400-pound body isn't exactly reminiscent of a Greek god, and his behavior in the ring is less than exemplary. As his name suggests, he is not above picking his nose.

Sex and Violence

Until recent years, women rarely appeared at wrestling events, but in the past decade, many male wrestlers have come to the ring accompanied by attractive women in revealing outfits. The women, often the wrestler's wife or girlfriend, pose as valets or even managers. Their main purpose is to add sex appeal for male fans. Extreme Championship Wrestling has gone so far as to feature adult film stars, such as Jasmin St. Claire, at its events.

1. ELIZABETH

Miss Elizabeth has been a fixture in professional wrestling since 1986. The ex-wife of The Macho Man Randy Savage, she served as his manager. The delicately attractive brunette rarely interfered in a match, but occasionally distracted Savage's opponents with her beauty. Unlike most women in wrestling, Elizabeth was modest and ladylike, but in 2000, she was forced to wrestle in WCW and even decked Madusa with a chair.

2. SUNNY

Sunny was one of the first WWF sex symbols. A video of Sunny posing in swimsuits was aired on a wrestling broadcast and fans downloaded more than a million of her photos on the Internet. Also known as Tammy Sytch, she managed the Bodydonnas, Skip and Zip, to the WWF tag-team title in 1996, but later switched allegiance to a rival team, The Smoking Gunns. She delighted in humiliating the country bumpkin Phineas Godwinn, who was lovesick for her. He sometimes lost matches when distracted by Sunny. She has also managed The Legion of Doom.

3. KIMBERLY

Kimberly Page is a stunning brunette who became World Championship Wrestling's answer to Sable. The wife of champion wrestler Diamond Dallas Page, she was first featured as his valet, The Diamond Doll. The shapely Mrs. Page appeared in a *Playboy* pictorial. She became the leader of The Nitro Girls dance team. Recently, Kimberly turned against her husband and became obsessed with promoting her own career. On one telecast, she was spanked by her angry husband.

4. FRANCINE

Francine rules as The Queen of Extreme Championship Wrestling. She has served as the "head cheerleader" for many wrestlers, including Shane Douglas. In 2000, she managed Justin Credible to the ECW world title.

5. TERRI RUNNELS

Terri Runnels was first seen in 1990 as Alexandra York, an accountant for money-conscious wrestler Mike Rotundo. In the World Wrestling Federation she let her hair down as Marlena, the cigar-smoking "director" of Goldust. In real life, she was married to Dustin Runnels (Goldust).

The Marlena character was nearly as kinky as Goldust. Brian Pillman and Goldust wrestled in a series of matches in which the winner took home Marlena. When Dustin Runnels dropped the Goldust character, Terri Runnels also started going by her real name. However, she continues to be involved in sexually explicit story lines. She supposedly became pregnant by Val Venis but lost the baby after she fell during a match.

6. MISSY HYATT

One of the first women to assume a prominent role in wrestling, Missy Hyatt was frequently seen in broadcasts in the 1980s. The pretty blonde assumed the role of a socialite, complete with low-cut gowns, white gloves, and diamond jewelry. She served as the valet to "Hot Stuff" Eddie Gilbert and was married to him in real life. She once flattened Hollywood John Tatum by hitting him over the head with her "loaded" Gucci handbag.

7. DAWN MARIE

Like Francine, Dawn Marie is a sexy brunette who made her reputation in the ECW. Dawn Marie is Extreme Championship Wrestling's bad girl. She has been manager to several ECW stars, most notably Tommy Dreamer.

8. THE KAT

The Kat, formerly known as Miss Kitty, has bared her claws (and other parts of her anatomy) during her stay in the

World Wrestling Federation. The protégé of Jerry "The King" Lawler, she opened eyes by showing her "puppies" on a pay-per-view broadcast. Not afraid of a good cat fight, she won the WWF women's title in December 1999.

9. **TRISH STRATUS**

A newcomer to the WWF, Trish Stratus leads the tag team T & A to the ring. Although T & A refers to the wrestlers Test and Albert, the name certainly has a double meaning. The chesty blonde makes her entrance wearing a hat, low-cut short dress, and a long black coat. Her low point came when she was the unlucky recipient of a "Stink Face" administered by Rikishi.

10. **BABY DOLL**

During the 1980s, Baby Doll earned the reputation of being the valet of champions. The tall blonde allied herself with some of the NWA's biggest stars: Ric Flair, Dusty Rhodes, Magnum T.A., and Tully Blanchard.

Queens of the Ring

Although women wrestlers have never been as popular as their male counterparts, they have a long history in the sport. In the 1930s, Gladys "Kill 'Em" Gillem wrestled alligators when she couldn't find a match with another female wrestler. Over the years, stars such as Vivian Vachon, Joyce Grable, Penny Banner, and Vicki Williams have proven that women can wrestle as well as men.

1. **THE FABULOUS MOOLAH**

Perhaps no athlete has dominated a sport to the extent that The Fabulous Moolah dominated women's professional wrestling. As Lillian Ellison, she began wrestling more than fifty years ago. In the early 1950s, she was Slave Girl Moolah, valet for The Elephant Boy and Nature Boy Buddy Rogers. By 1956, The Fabulous Moolah had won the women's title, and she held the belt until 1984 when she was finally defeated by Wendi Richter. She recaptured the title posing as a masked wrestler, The Spider Lady. The ageless one last won the WWF ladies' title in 1999.

2. CHYNA

Chyna, "The Ninth Wonder of the World," doesn't need to wrestle for the women's title. The 200-pound bodybuilder is more than a match for most male wrestlers. Chyna became the first woman to win the Intercontinental title in 1999 and was later a co-holder of the belt with Chris Jericho. She appeared in a *Playboy* pictorial in 2000.

3. WENDI RICHTER

Wendi Richter will forever be remembered by wrestling fans as the woman who defeated The Fabulous Moolah. Managed by rock star Cyndi Lauper, The Texas Cowgirl won the WWF women's title in 1984.

4. MADUSA

Probably the most successful woman wrestler of the past decade, Madusa Miceli combines technical prowess and kick-boxing skills. She has won women's world titles wherever she has wrestled. As Alundra Blaze, she won the WWF women's title three times between 1993 and 1995. In 1999, she became the first woman to win the WCW cruiserweight title.

5. SABLE

Sable may not have been the greatest woman wrestler in history, but she certainly was the most striking. The blonde bombshell was introduced to wrestling fans as a ring girl for Hunter Hearst Helmsley and her husband, Marvelous Marc Mero. She created a sensation when she wore a skimpy outfit at the 1997 Slammy Awards. Soon thereafter, Rena Mero entered the wrestling ring as Sable. She showed surprising skills and developed her own finishing move called The

Sable

Dr. Mike Lano

Sable's sex appeal has caused quite a stir among wrestling fans, never more so than when she took on Jacqueline in the now-famous bikini match.

Sablebomb. Sable won the WWF women's title in 1998. Naturally, her sex appeal was exploited whenever possible. Sales of *Playboy* skyrocketed when she did her nude pictorials. She left little to the imagination in a bikini match against Jacqueline. Sable wowed the audience with a painted-on bikini.

6. SHERRI MARTEL

Sherri Martel excelled as both a wrestler and manager. She was one of the top women wrestlers of the 1980s and won title belts in nearly every federation in which she appeared. A highlight of her career was winning the WWF women's championship in 1987. Sensational Sherri also managed the AWA world tag-team champs Pretty Boy Doug Somers and Playboy Buddy Rose.

7. MILDRED BURKE

Mildred Burke was the first great woman wrestler. In the 1930s she toured the country, challenging men to wrestle her. She wrestled against more than 200 men and was defeated only once. Burke dominated the early years of women's professional wrestling.

8. JACQUELINE

Jacqueline has been a star in both World Championship Wrestling and the World Wrestling Federation. In the WCW she defeated male wrestlers such as Disco Inferno and managed Harlem Heat to the WCW tag-team title. After moving to the World Wrestling Federation, she defeated Sable for the women's title in 1998 and won it a second time two years later.

9. **DEBRA MCMICHAEL**

Granted, she isn't much of a wrestler, but lack of wrestling skills didn't stop Debra McMichael from winning the WWF women's title in May 1999. She had apparently lost a night-gown match when WWF officials decided to strip Sable of her title and award it to Debra. The former wife of Chicago Bears' great Steve "Mongo" McMichael, Debra was once crowned Miss Illinois and Miss Texas USA.

10. **G.L.O.W.**

The Gorgeous Ladies of Wrestling (G.L.O.W.) was a Las Vegas-based promotion of the 1980s that had to be seen to be believed. The roster of women wrestlers included The Evil Russian, Colonel Ninotchka, The Cheerleader, Americana, the blonde California Doll, Tina Ferrari, Palestina, the huge Mathilda the Hun, and the even larger Mountain Fiji. Among the nobable tag teams were The Soul Patrol, Adore and Envie, Hollywood and Vine, and The Heavy Metal Sisters, Chainsaw and Spike.

Captain Lou Albano

Captain Lou was a successful wrestler in his own right before he became one of the best-known managers and made a memorable cameo appearance as Cyndi Lauper's overbearing father in the music video "Girls Just Want to Have Fun."

Managers of Champions

A good wrestling manager can be the difference between winning and losing a match. One of their tricks is to distract the referee while their wrestler does something illegal. Managers frequently interfere in matches, often deciding the outcome.

1. CAPTAIN LOU ALBANO

Before he became a manager, Captain Lou Albano was a successful tag-team wrestler. In 1967, he and Tony Altimore won the WWF tag-team title. Two years later, Captain Lou Albano began a career in which he managed more than ten world tag-team champions. Two of his most successful teams were The Moondogs and The Headshrinkers. Albano also managed Ivan Koloff to the WWF title in 1971, when the Russian ended Bruno Sammartino's eight-year reign as champion.

2. THE GRAND WIZARD OF WRESTLING

One of wrestling's most outstanding and outrageous managers was The Grand Wizard of Wrestling. Also known as

Abdullah Farouk, he dressed in a turban, loud sportcoats, shiny boots, and wraparound sunglasses. Over the years, The Wizard managed many of wrestling's most hated villains: The Sheik, Ernie Ladd, Superstar Billy Graham, Stan Stasiak, and Greg Valentine, to name a few. The Grand Wizard, whose real name was Ernie Roth, passed away in 1983.

3. JIMMY HART

Perhaps no wrestling manager has represented so many superstars as Jimmy Hart. The "Mouth of the South" managed Hulk Hogan, Randy Savage, The Giant, Lex Luger, King Kong Bundy, The Honky Tonk Man, and many others.

4. PAUL BEARER

Unlike most successful managers, Paul Bearer rarely interferes in his wrestlers' matches. He guided The Undertaker to the WWF world title in 1991. Paul Bearer held a bronze urn that gave The Undertaker a mysterious power. He became the host of an interview segment on the WWF broadcasts called "The Funeral Parlor." When The Undertaker's "brother," Kane, arrived in the World Wrestling Federation, Paul Bearer became his manager. He claimed that the giant Kane was his son. In his previous life as a manager, he was known as Percy Pringle.

5. HARVEY WIPPLEMAN

Harvey Wippleman was a small, bespectacled man in a seersucker suit. He liked to talk big and had the wrestlers to back him up. When he was managing Sid Justice, Wippleman would climb into the ring after the match with a stethoscope and check the unconscious opponent for signs of life.

6. BOBBY "THE BRAIN" HEENAN

Before he became an announcer, Bobby "The Brain" Heenan was one of the sport's most successful and hated managers. He referred to the fans as "humanoids" and "ham and eggers." Rather than being called a manager, The Brain referred to himself as a financial advisor. He assured his wrestlers that he was properly handling their money, but everyone doubted his sincerity. He managed Nick Bockwinkel during his reigns as the AWA world champion. Other stars he managed included Blackjack Mulligan, Jimmy Valiant, Ivan Koloff, Baron Von Raschke, and Lord Alfred Hayes.

7. "CLASSY" FREDDIE BLASSIE

Fred Blassie was one of many top wrestlers to also become premier managers. For forty years he was one of wrestling's most despised heels. He called fans and his opponents "pencil-neck geeks." As a manager, he chose to represent a new generation of villains: Big John Studd, Jesse Ventura, Stan Hansen, Adrian Adonis, Spiros Arion, and Killer Khan. He prided himself in managing only the meanest wrestlers. Blassie managed Hulk Hogan when he first arrived in the World Wrestling Federation. In 1983, Blassie's Iron Sheik defeated Bob Backlund for the WWF title. When Muhammad Ali fought wrestler Antonio Inoki, he selected Fred Blassie as his trainer. Blassie remarked that he'd have his wrestlers hit their own mothers if it meant winning a match.

8. EDDIE CRECHMAN

Eddie Crechman was one of the most irritating managers in wrestling history. Crechman wore black-rimmed glasses and had a grating voice. The manager of The Sheik during the

1960s and 1970s, he taunted his opponents throughout the matches. Because The Sheik did not speak English, Crechman served as his mouthpiece.

9. ARNOLD SKAALAND

Known as "The Golden Boy" during his long wrestling career, Arnold Skaaland became the manager of champions in the World Wrestling Federation. Skaaland managed Bruno Sammartino and Bob Backlund, two wrestlers who held the WWF championship belts almost continuously between 1963 and 1984. Unlike most managers, Skaaland behaved like a gentleman and almost never interfered in his wrestlers' matches.

10. GENERAL ADNAN

As Sheik Adnan El Kaissey, he was one of the most hated wrestlers in the American Wrestling Association. The sheik from Iraq claimed to have contempt for everything American. He used his great wealth to buy the contracts of many top wrestlers in the federation. Among the wrestlers in his stable were Crusher Blackwell, Abdullah the Butcher, King Kong Bundy, and Ken Patera. In the early 1990s, he emerged in the WWF as General Adnan, a military mastermind from Iraq who was instrumental in convincing Sergeant Slaughter to turn against his country. Slaughter won the WWF title in 1991 from The Ultimate Warrior. When he lost it to Hulk Hogan two months later, he was savagely attacked by General Adnan.

Million-Dollar Men

As in most professions, money is very important in wrestling. To some wrestlers and managers, it's the most important thing.

1. THE MILLION DOLLAR MAN

Ted DiBiase was an excellent technical wrestler whose career took off when he became known as The Million Dollar Man. DiBiase claimed to have mansions all over the world, a fleet of luxury cars, and a staff of French-trained chefs. His valet, Virgil, attended to his every wish. He wore boots with money signs on them. In the ring he finished off opponents with a sleeper hold he called "The Million Dollar Dream." After matches he stuffed hundred-dollar bills into the mouths of incapacitated foes. "Everyone has a price," he said, and demonstrated this by having fans do degrading things such as kissing his feet for money. He and Irwin R. Schyster formed a tag team called Money, Inc. and won the WWF title three times in 1992 and 1993.

2. **MICHAEL WALLSTREET**

In one of his many incarnations, Mike Rotundo became Michael Wallstreet. The character was based on the corporate raider, Gordon Gecko, played by Michael Douglas in the 1987 film, *Wall Street*. With his slicked-back hair, Wallstreet bore a striking resemblance to Douglas.

3. **BIG MONEY HANK JAMES**

One of the first wrestlers to use money to antagonize fans was Big Money Hank James in the early 1970s. Calling himself "The Champagne and Diamond Man," James claimed that he spent his spare time counting money. He said that he had money trees growing in his yard. James told his opponents that he wouldn't humiliate them in the ring if they gave him all their money. His catch phrase was, "All I want is your money, Honey."

4. **ANDY KAUFMAN**

During his feud with wrestler Jerry "The King" Lawler, comedian Andy Kaufman appeared on *The David Letterman Show*. After Lawler slapped him, Kaufman unleashed a torrent of obscenities. It was hinted that NBC was considering banning him from appearing on the network. Kaufman threatened to sue NBC for $200 million. If he won the suit, he promised to buy NBC and turn it into an all-wrestling network.

5. **BIG JOHN STUDD**

At six feet, nine inches tall and weighing 365 pounds, Big John Studd lived up to his name. He was so confident that no one was strong enough to body slam him that he offered

$10,000 to any wrestler who could perform the feat. After many unsuccessful attempts, Andre the Giant met Studd in a $15,000 winner-take-all body-slam match. Andre became the first man to body slam Studd and began tossing the money to the crowd. Studd's manager, Bobby "The Brain" Heenan, retrieved as many dollars as he could and ran off with the gym bag full of money.

6. ANDRE THE GIANT

On February 5, 1988, Andre The Giant pinned Hulk Hogan to win the WWF world title for the first time. Fans were shocked when Andre gave the belt to The Million Dollar Man Ted DiBiase. It turned out that DiBiase had paid off the referees and had given Andre a large sum of money for the belt DiBiase was unable to win on his own. WWF President Jack Tunney declared the title vacant and DiBiase was forced to return the belt he coveted so much. DiBiase was so incensed that he had his own Million Dollar Belt made for himself.

7. E.Z. MONEY

In the summer of 2000, a wrestler appeared in Extreme Championship Wrestling who was literally covered in cash. E.Z. Money's wrestling trunks, elbow pads, kneepads, and boots had dollar bills sticking out of them.

8. THE MILLIONAIRE'S CLUB

Some of the World Championship Wrestling's most established stars formed The Millionaire's Club in the year 2000. The exclusive club consisted of Ric Flair, Diamond Dallas Page, Hulk Hogan, and Sting. They were opposed by a group of wrestlers, headed by Vampiro, known as The New Blood.

9. **DIAMOND DALLAS PAGE**

Early in his career, Diamond Dallas Page was depicted as a multi-millionaire. In 1996, Page supposedly lost his $6 million fortune and was reduced to selling his wrestling attire to up-and-coming wrestlers.

10. **JESSE VENTURA**

During his successful run for governor of Minnesota in 1998, Jesse Ventura aired a series of clever low-budget commercials. In one of those ads, a Jesse Ventura action figure was approached by a "Special Interest Man" doll and offered a dime. Ventura returned the money, demonstrating that he could not be bought by special interest groups.

Whose Side Are You On?

Professional wrestling has always divided its performers into good scientific wrestlers called babyfaces and bad rulebreakers known as heels. To keep the storylines fresh, it is often necessary to have wrestlers change their image. Few wrestlers spend their entire careers as babyfaces or heels. In recent years, the line between heroes and villains has been clouded.

1. HULK HOGAN

Early in his career, wrestling under the name of Sterling Golden, Hulk Hogan was a bad guy. When he returned to the WWF in 1983, he was the ultimate role model for his young fans. He told them that if they wanted to grow up to be like him they needed to say their prayers and take their vitamins. From 1984 to 1993, Hogan won the WWF world title five times. When he signed with rival World Championship Wrestling in 1994, he was still the personification of the wrestling hero. However, two years later, he unexpectedly became the leader of The New World Order, a group of heels that included Kevin Nash and Scott Hall. The goal of the NWO was to take over World Championship Wrestling. Hogan exchanged the famed yellow tights of his Hulkamania days for the black tights of The New World Order. He rechristened himself Hollywood Hogan and boasted of his film career. By 2000, Hogan had returned to his good-guy ways.

2. STONE COLD STEVE AUSTIN

When Steve Austin came to the World Wrestling Federation in the mid-1990s, he developed a persona that would make him a superstar. He saw a film about a serial killer called The Ice Man. He believed a cold-blooded character would give him the edge he needed to stand out from other WWF stars. His wife, Jeannie, came up with the name "Stone Cold." His new hell-raiser attitude was a hit with fans. When Austin wrestled good guy Bret Hart, he was surprised to see many fans rooting for him even though he was a heel. His "I don't give a damn" attitude made him an anti-hero. He solidified his position as a fan favorite when he feuded with the unpopular head of the World Wrestling Federation, Vince McMahon. The Texas Rattlesnake didn't even have to change his ways to become one of the most popular wrestlers in history.

3. BOB BACKLUND

Before he became a professional wrestler, Bob Backlund won the NCAA wrestling title in 1971. The four-time All American used his superior wrestling knowledge to win the WWF world title from Superstar Billy Graham in 1978. He held the title for more than five years. When Backlund finally lost the belt to The Iron Sheik, the promoter suggested that he become a heel. Backlund resisted the change and retired from wrestling, but by the time he returned to the WWF in the early 1990s, a shift in his attitude was apparent. He seemed to lose his mind after a loss to Bret Hart in 1994.

Backlund berated the fans for not supporting him and failing to live up to his high standards. He began interfering in other matches, applying his dreaded Cross-Faced Chicken Wing hold. Now hated by the fans, he recaptured the WWF title in November 1994, only to lose it a few days later to Diesel.

4. **RODDY PIPER**

Roddy Piper has always been the perfect villain, yet he has spent much of his career as a fan favorite. In the early 1980s he was the archnemesis of NWA fan favorite Ric Flair. He continued to be the promotion's biggest heel until one day the announcer told fans that Piper had saved some children from a knife-wielding assailant. Although Piper's rough-house style and smart aleck demeanor had not changed, he was suddenly popular with the fans. In 1984, he switched to the World Wrestling Federation, became the rival of Hulk Hogan, and was once again the most despised man in wrestling. Piper was so entertaining that within a few years he had the fans back on his side. In 1996, Piper defeated Hogan at the WCW Starcade pay-per-view. This time Piper was the babyface and Hogan the heel.

5. **PETER MAIVIA**

High Chief Peter Maivia was a popular star of the World Wrestling Federation. In 1978, the colorful Samoan teamed up with champion Bob Backlund in a match against two rule breakers, Victor Rivera and Spiros Arion. Maivia had always been a scientific wrestler, so fans were horrified when he attacked Backlund's manager Arnold Skaaland and then Backlund himself. A few months later, he did the same thing to another tag-team partner, Chief Jay Strongbow. It turned out that Maivia's sudden change was the result of large payments from his manager, Fred Blassie.

6. LEX LUGER

Lex Luger's magnificent physique has always been his greatest asset. For most of his early years in World Championship Wrestling, he was a fan favorite. In 1991, he won the WCW world title for the first time. Two years later, he debuted in the World Wrestling Federation. No longer "The Total Package," Luger was known as "The Narcissist." His vanity made him an instant heel. Later that year, Luger regained fan support when he body slammed the 600-pound Yokozuna. The Total Package was repackaged as "Made in the USA," an American hero.

7. KEN PATERA

Ken Patera won a bronze medal in weightlifting for the United States at the 1972 Olympics. During his early years in professional wrestling, he was a scientific wrestler. Frustrated at being passed over for title shots, he hired Lou Albano as his manager. Albano taught him to win at all costs. Patera's philosophy can be summed up by his motto: "Win if you can, lose if you must, but always cheat."

8. KURT ANGLE

Kurt Angle won the gold medal in the 220-pound freestyle event at the 1996 Olympics. Ordinarily, his achievement should have made him an instant fan favorite. However, when he entered the WWF, he billed himself as "Your American Hero." His self-righteous attitude immediately rubbed fans the wrong way. In February 2000, he won both the Intercontinental and European championships, which did nothing to check his ego. Later that year, Angle won the World Wrestling Federation heavyweight title.

Dr. Mike Lano

Superfly Jimmy Snuka

One of yesteryear's stars, Superfly Jimmy Snuka is still admired by today's young fans.

9. JIMMY SNUKA

Jimmy Snuka is a classic example of a wrestler whose ability was so spectacular that he became a babyface without trying. The Superfly engaged in a series of WWF world-title matches with champion Bob Backlund in 1982. Snuka's brutal tactics nearly earned him the world title, but it was his amazing aerial skills that won the hearts of fans. Soon, Superfly Jimmy Snuka was one of the most popular wrestlers in the World Wrestling Federation.

10. BRET HART

Bret Hart was one of the most decorated stars in WWF history. "The Hitman" held the WWF world title five times between 1992 and 1997 and won a tag-team belt as a member of the Hart Foundation in 1987 with partner Jim "The Anvil" Neidhart. Hart prided himself on projecting a positive image to his young fans, but by the late 1990s the Canadian superstar had become a heel after making disparaging remarks about American fans.

Multiple Personalities

M ost wrestlers have an identity crisis. Over the course of their careers, they will assume numerous personas. Here are ten wrestlers who have had more than their share of name changes.

1. MICK FOLEY

Mick Foley not only had multiple identities, he had them at the same time. During his peak years in the World Wrestling Federation in the late 1990s, he juggled four separate identities. For years, he had been Cactus Jack, a hardcore legend who liked to hurt people and liked to be hurt. His second personality was Mankind, a deranged individual who pulled out his own hair. He was also Dude Love, a hippie who dressed in tie-dyed tights. His fourth personality was himself, Mick Foley. Foley was so unstable that he once blamed bad tortilla chips for one of his personality changes.

2. GLENN JACOBS

Glenn Jacobs, now known as Kane, has had his share of unusual personas. The huge wrestler began as The Christmas Creature, Santa's largest elf. His next identity was only slightly better. As Unabom, he based his character on the well-known serial bomber. Next, he re-emerged as Isaac Yankem, the sadistic dentist. When Kevin Nash, then known as Diesel, jumped to the WCW, Jacobs tried to fill his boots as The New Diesel. Like New Coke, The New Diesel was short-lived. He finally found his true identity as Kane, The Undertaker's deformed brother, whose face is so hideous that he wears a mask.

3. SEAN WALTMAN

A decade ago, Sean Waltman debuted as The Lightning Kid. In his early days in the WWF, the Kid, barely 200 pounds, took his lumps. He appeared on three consecutive RAW broadcasts in 1993. Each week he had a different name. The first week he was The Lightning Kid. The next week he appeared as The Kamikaze Kid. The following week he was The Cannonball Kid. The results were always the same—he lost. In May 1992, the Kid defeated Razor Ramon in a huge upset. The victory earned him a new name, The 1-2-3 Kid. As a member of The New World Order, he was known as Syxx. His return to the WWF found him re-introduced as X-Pac. X-Pac joined another outlaw group, Degeneration X.

4. BRUTUS BEEFCAKE

Brutus Beefcake is one of the few wrestlers whose early identity was more successful than subsequent reincarnations. As

Brutus Beefcake, he and Greg Valentine won the WWF tag-team title in 1985. He was a headliner as Brutus "The Barber" Beefcake. Since then, he has been The Booty Man, The Butcher, Zodiac, and The Disciple, but he has never generated the excitement that he did as The Barber.

5. SCOTT HALL

Scott Hall would probably rather forget his early personas: Cowboy Scott Hall and Starship Coyote. In the early 1990s, he began to get attention in World Championship Wrestling as The Diamond Studd. Hall didn't become a star until 1993, when he won the Intercontinental title as Razor Ramon. "The Bad Guy" won that title three more times before returning to the WCW under his real name.

6. KEVIN NASH

Kevin Nash's career has followed a path similar to that of his friend, Scott Hall. Master Blaster Steele was inspired by a character in a Mad Max movie. Nash's most forgettable character was Oz, in which he portrayed a silver-haired wizard. His fortunes improved somewhat when he showed up in the WCW as bouncer Vinnie Vegas. Nash's rise to superstardom was capped off when, as Diesel, he destroyed Bob Backlund to win the WWF world heavyweight title. He used his real name when he became a charter member of The New World Order. Since then, "Big Sexy" has won the WCW world championship several times.

7. CHARLES WRIGHT

Who's Charles Wright? You may remember him as Papa Shango, the witch doctor who terrorized the WWF in the early

Kevin Nash

Dr. Mike Lano

Seven-foot bruiser "Big Sexy" Kevin Nash has achieved superstardom in recent years, but he had less successful stints in the past while wrestling under the names Master Blaster Steele, Oz, and Vinnie Vegas.

1990s. The voodoo master transformed into Kama Mustapha, member of The Nation of Domination. His most popular guise is The Godfather, wrestling's most successful pimp.

8. STEVE WILLIAMS

Steve Williams began wrestling under his real name. He was forced to change his ring name because it was already being used by the better-known Dr. Death Steve Williams. A promoter changed his name to Steve Austin, after the Lee Majors character in the television series, *The Six Million Dollar Man*. His first taste of success occurred in the WCW as the blonde-haired pretty boy, Stunning Steve Austin. In March 1993, he teamed with Brian Pillman to win the WCW tag-team title as The Hollywood Blonds. After his career stalled in World Championship Wrestling, he made a brief stop in the ECW as The Stevester. His WWF bow was equally inspiring. In 1995, he appeared as The Ringmaster, Ted DiBiase's so-called Million Dollar Champion. He had gone from being The Six Million Dollar Man to The Million Dollar Champion. Only after he changed his identity to Stone Cold Steve Austin in February 1996 did he become the superstar he is today.

9. BRIAN ARMSTRONG

Brian Armstrong, the son of famed wrestler Bob Armstrong, began his career as The Dark Secret in 1993. That identity, thankfully, remained a secret. The following year he debuted in the WWF as Jeff Jarrett's assistant, The Roadie. His elevation to stardom came as Jesse James, a member of The New Age Outlaws tag team. As Jesse James, he won the Intercontinental title in 1999. He has reached a new high in popularity as The Road Dogg.

10. **RANDY SAVAGE**

Randy Savage has won both the WWF and WCW world titles as The Macho Man. He has wrestled under the name Randy Savage for nearly a quarter of a century. Wrestling trivia buffs may recall that his early aliases included The Spider, The Executioner, and The Destroyer.

Thank You, Masked Men

M asked wrestlers have always added an air of mystery to the sport. The first was The Masked Wrestler of Paris in 1873. In the United States, wrestlers actually wore masks to hide their identities. Their opponents frequently spent so much time trying to unmask them that they lost the matches.

1. MIL MASCARAS

The most famous masked wrestler of all time was the Mexican sensation, Mil Mascaras. The Man of a Thousand Masks confounded his opponents with his aerial scientific wrestling prowess. Although he never won a major world title, he was a superstar all over the globe.

2. EL SANTO

One of the few masked wrestlers who could rival Mil Mascaras for popularity in Mexico was El Santo. He was Mexico's most popular wrestler for two decades, but gained even greater fame as the country's top box-office attraction. He starred in more than 60 films, usually campy horror movies in which he battled monsters. Some of his best-known films include *Santo vs. Frankenstein's Daughter, Santo vs. the Martian Invasion, Santo Against the Zombies,* and the wrestler/monster tag-team epic *Santo and the Blue Demon vs. Dracula and the Wolfman.* When El Santo died in 1984, he was buried in his beloved silver mask.

3.   THE SUPER DESTROYER

The Super Destroyer lived up to his name in the 1970s. The 280-pound masked man wore a black glove which seemed to make his claw hold even more devastating. He frequently finished off opponents by leaping from the top rope onto their throats.

4.   JUSHIN THUNDER LIGER

Jushin Liger has won junior heavyweight titles all over the world. The Japanese masked star won the WWF light-heavyweight belt in 1997. The high-flyer has invented several holds, including the shooting-star press.

5.   THE MASKED SUPERSTAR

The Masked Superstar was one of the AWA's top stars of the 1980s. The 290-pounder wore stars on his mask and tights. It was said that he wore a mask because he had hurt so many wrestlers in the past that no one would wrestle him if they knew his identity.

6.   MR. WRESTLING II

Mr. Wrestling II was one of the most popular masked wrestlers of the 1970s. He and Mr Wrestling I (Tim Woods) formed one of the best tag teams of the decade. Unlike most masked wrestlers of the time, Mr. Wrestling II was a purely scientific grappler. One of his biggest fans was Lillian Carter, mother of President Jimmy Carter. Miss Lillian even invited the masked man to her home.

7. SHARK BOY

This masked man has a rabid following in the Midwest. Shark Boy has won a number of regional cruiserweight titles. He wears a mask with big teeth and a shark fin on top. On occasion, he has been known to bite the backsides of opponents. His finisher is The Dead Sea Drop.

8. CAT BURGLAR

The Cat Burglar wrestled when he was supposedly on furlough from the Maryland State Penitentiary. As you might have guessed, he had been sent to the big house for burglary. In the ring, he wore a mask to conceal his identity and gloves so he wouldn't leave any fingerprints.

9. THE MASKED TERROR

The Masked Terror cut a bloody path through the Midwest. He seemed unbeatable until he was pinned and unmasked by Dick the Bruiser in Cincinnati in 1964. He turned out to be a bearded wrestler known as The Alaskan.

10. THE MASKED CANADIAN

In the mid-1970s, future superstar Roddy Piper wrestled in California. To supplement his income, he wrestled both as Roddy Piper and as The Masked Canadian, often on the same card. Amazingly, The Masked Canadian was more popular at the time than The Rowdy Scot. Piper was born in Scotland and raised in Canada.

Dr. Mike Lano

Sting

The only thing more chilling than Sting's phantom face paint is his signature Scorpion Death Lock.

The Roar of the Face Paint

In the past decade, many wrestlers have begun wearing face paint. Unlike a mask, face paint does not inhibit a wrestler's sight or breathing and can be changed for each match.

1. **STING**

Sting has been one of the most dependable and successful wrestlers in World Championship Wrestling. While other wrestlers have jumped to other federations, Sting has remained loyal to the WCW and won its world championship belt six times between 1992 and 1999. The Stinger's trademark is his ever-changing face paint. Sting's face paint often matches the color of his tights. His all-white phantom facial mask is usually worn when he is dressed in all black.

2. **THE ULTIMATE WARRIOR**

The Ultimate Warrior was one of the first wrestling superstars to wear face paint. He began wearing the paint as The Dingo Warrior in the mid-1980s. His warrior makeup was an integral part of his character. In 1990, The Ultimate Warrior defeated Hulk Hogan to win the WWF world title.

3. THE LEGION OF DOOM

Arguably the greatest tag team of all time, The Legion of Doom intimidated opponents with their spiked Road Warrior vests, their roughhouse style, and their ever-changing face paint. Hawk and Animal wore black, white, and red face paint that complemented their mohawk and reverse mohawk hairstyles.

4. THE GREAT KABUKI

The Great Kabuki was wrestling's man of mystery. The martial-arts expert was a top draw in the NWA in the 1980s. He wore hideous face paint and spewed a green mist into his opponents' eyes.

5. THE HEADHUNTERS

The Headhunters have earned their reputation as one of the most dangerous tag teams in professional wrestling. Although The Headhunters weighed over 400 pounds each, they were capable of crushing their opponents with a moonsault. The pair looked even more fearsome because they wore black and white war paint.

6. KEVIN SULLIVAN

Pro wrestling's satanic majesty, Kevin Sullivan enhanced his demonic image by wearing face paint. He sometimes painted an "X" on his forehead or painted one side of his face black and the other white.

7. ADRIAN STREET

For Adrian Street, wearing face paint was a fashion statement. "The Exotic One" was appalled by his opponents' lack of style. Street's outrageous makeup and unconventional hairstyle caused some to refer to him as "The Boy George of Wrestling."

8. THE ICEMAN

The Iceman was a popular wrestler in Canada during the late 1990s. He wore white face paint to emphasize his icy nature.

9. KENDO NAGASAKI

The Ninja Warrior Kendo Nagasaki was one of the more frightening wrestlers of the 1980s, for opponents and fans alike. The martial-arts specialist painted his face in garish colors. As his name suggests, he frequently used a Kendo stick as a weapon.

10. SHERRI MARTEL

Men aren't the only wrestlers to wear face paint. Sherri Martel, a champion wrestler and manager of champions, wore face paint to reflect her moods. The makeup could be anything: tears, a heart, or a decorative design.

Kings of the Ring

The number of monarchs around the world may be dwindling, but there's no shortage of wrestling royalty.

1. LORD ALFRED HAYES

Lord Alfred Hayes claimed to be an English nobleman, born across the street from the House of Lords. A wrestler from the 1950s to the 1970s, Hayes referred to his manager Bobby Heenan as a gentleman's gentleman. He called his finishing move, a half-nelson, "London Bridge." Hayes gained even greater fame as an affable announcer on WWF broadcasts in the 1980s.

2. JERRY "THE KING" LAWLER

Jerry "The King" Lawler always wore a crown on his way to the ring. Over the years he has been the king of most federations in which he wrestled. Lawler won the AWA world title in 1988 and has held the United States Wrestling Association heavyweight title an incredible twenty-six times.

For the last several years, the King has been the color announcer on WWF broadcasts, although he occasionally wrestles. In June 2000, he defeated Dean Malenko in an "over the top-top off" match. Lawler represented The Kat while Malenko wrestled on behalf of Terri Runnels. Every time Lawler or Malenko was tossed over the top rope, his sexy partner would have to remove an article of clothing. This combination of a battle royal and striptease was won by Jerry Lawler. Just as Terri was about to remove her top, wrestler Stevie Richards covered her with a sign that read "censored," much to the disappointment of the audience.

3. LORD ATHOL LAYTON

The Canadian-born wrestler was known for his dignified manner. During the 1960s, Lord Layton became a successful wrestling announcer in the Midwest. He was appalled by the brutal tactics of wrestlers like The Sheik and sometimes interfered in the matches to save the unfortunate opponent from further punishment.

4. KING TONGA

King Tonga was one of the biggest heels in the AWA in the 1980s. He frequently acted as a bounty hunter, paid to put wrestlers out of action. He combined martial-arts skills with illegal tactics.

5. SIR OLIVER HUMPERDINK

No relation to Englebert, Sir Oliver Humperdink was a manager in the 1980s who was despised by most American fans for his arrogant manner and interfering in his wrestlers' matches. Ironically, Sir Oliver was really from Florida.

6. BARON VON RASCHKE

Baron Von Raschke was the master of The German Claw, a hold which won him hundreds of matches. The Baron also used a neck-breaker hold which he called The Hangman. A hated rule breaker early in his career, he became a fan favorite in his later years. He teamed with The Crusher to win the AWA world tag-team title in 1983.

7. BARON MIKEL SCICLUNA

Another baron who could be a royal pain to opponents and fans alike was Mikel Scicluna, from the isle of Malta. He was particularly skilled in tag-team bouts, having shared the WWF world tag-team belts with Smasher Sloan in 1966 and King Curtis in 1972.

8. BARON MICHEL LEONE

Baron Michel Leone won many titles on the West Coast during the 1950s. Leone also held the NWA world junior heavyweight championship.

9. PRINCE IAUKEA

In February 1997, newcomer Prince Iaukea challenged Lord Steven Regal for the WCW television title. The Hawaiian prince upset the English lord to win the belt. The victory propelled him to rookie-of-the-year honors.

10. KING KURT ANGLE

The World Wrestling Federation stages an annual pay-per-view event called *The King of the Ring.* The 2000 winner was former Olympic gold medalist Kurt Angle. The next evening on RAW, the WWF Monday night telecast, King Kurt walked to the ring wearing a crown. His coronation was spoiled when Shawn Michaels destroyed his throne and Hunter Hearst Helmsley decked Angle and threw him out of the ring.

The British Are Coming

Wrestlers from the British Isles have ranged from superior ring technicians, such as Steven Regal, to brawlers such as Fit Finlay.

1. THE BRITISH BULLDOG

Davey Boy Smith, The British Bulldog, has been a powerhouse in professional wrestling for more than fifteen years. He and The Dynamite Kid formed the tag team The British Bulldogs. The Bulldogs defeated Greg Valentine and Brutus Beefcake at Wrestlemania II in 1986 to win the WWF tag-team title. In 1992, Smith captured the Intercontinental title. Five years later, The British Bulldog became the first WWF European champion.

2. BILLY ROBINSON

Billy Robinson wrestled throughout the world. The former British Empire champion was a perennial contender for the AWA world title. He shared the AWA world tag-team title with Verne Gagne in 1972 and with The Crusher in 1973.

3. **LORD STEVEN REGAL**

Lord Steven Regal could never hide his contempt for the fans, whom he considered commoners. An excellent mat technician, he won the WCW television title four times between 1993 and 1997. He formed The Blue Bloods tag team with Bobby Eaton.

4. **CHRIS ADAMS**

Gentleman Chris Adams was one of the top wrestlers in World Class Wrestling in Texas during the 1980s. Accompanied by his blonde companion, Sunshine, Adams engaged in a spirited feud with Kerry von Erich. Stone Cold Steve Austin was a graduate of Adams's wrestling school.

5. **SCREAMIN' NORMAN SMILEY**

A native of London, Norman Smiley became the first WCW hardcore champion in 1999. The eccentric wrestler surprised his opponents by wearing protective gear such as a football helmet. He got his nickname by letting out piercing screams during his matches.

6. **AXL ROTTEN**

The 300-pound Brit is known for his brutality in the ring. Rotten uses steel chairs for more than sitting. He has taken part in some of the most barbaric matches in wrestling history, including barbed-wire baseball bat matches and bouts in which he was showered with thumbtacks. He formed a memorable tag team in Extreme Championship Wrestling with Balls Mahoney.

7. IAN ROTTEN

Nearly as rotten as his brother Axl, Ian Rotten is another hardcore specialist. No match is too violent for him. He competed in a match in which his taped fists were covered with broken glasses. His feud with Madman Pondo has resulted in numerous bloodbaths.

8. BLACK ANGUS

Black Angus was a popular wrestler in the 1970s. A favorite in the Southwest, the bearded Scot had feuds with Blackjack Mulligan and Blackjack Lanza.

9. LORD BLEARS

Lord Blears was the prototype of the snooty English nobleman in professional wrestling. Blears was a star in the 1940s and 1950s.

10. FIT FINLAY

Known for his toughness and willingness to brawl, David "Fit" Finlay was called The Belfast Bruiser. He got into the sport because his father was a promoter in Ireland. In 1998, Finlay defeated Booker T to win the WCW world TV title.

German Grapplers

For a long time after World War II, German wrestlers were stereotyped as bald, goose-stepping Nazis. These cruel rule breakers were some of wrestling's most hated villains of the 1950s and 1960s.

1. FRITZ VON ERICH

Fritz von Erich was one of the most successful German stars. In reality, he was Jack Adkisson, a former football star from Southern Methodist University. In 1963, he won the American Wrestling Association world heavyweight title. His Iron Claw hold caused wrestlers to quickly submit or pass out. The claw was so devastating that it was banned in several states. When his wrestling days were over, he became a respected promoter in Texas. His sons, Kerry and Kevin, were also champions.

2. HANS SCHMIDT

Another German star of the 1960s was Hans Schmidt. The evil Schmidt often used his riding crop as a weapon.

3. **HANS HERMANN**

Hans Hermann was a German heel of the 1950s. He was particularly effective in tag-team matches. His tag partners included Killer Kowalski and Fritz von Erich.

4. **WALDO VON ERICH**

Unrelated to Fritz, Waldo von Erich starred in the United States and abroad in the 1970s. He wore a German helmet into the ring. His finishing maneuver was The Blitzkrieg Drop from the top rope.

5. **BERLYN**

He debuted as Alex Wright in 1994. Anyone who ever saw the young German dance his way into the ring almost wished for the days of the goose-stepping wrestlers. A few years ago, Wright transformed himself into Berlyn, a bald, bearded wrestler with a bad attitude. His goal is to humiliate Americans and take the WCW title back to Germany.

6. **KILLER KARL KRUPP**

Killer Karl Krupp's specialty was the claw hold. While most wrestlers apply their claws to the face or forehead, Krupp had claw holds for all parts of the body. He applied face claws, eye claws, and stomach claws, but his favorite was the armpit claw. Krupp's tag-team partners included Kurt von Steiger and Killer Karl Kox.

7. **KURT VON HESS**

Kurt von Hess also excelled in tag-team action. Hess teamed with Al Costello, formerly of The Fabulous Kangaroos, in a team called The Internationals. Another favorite partner was

Karl von Shotz. They formed the tag team known as The Aryans. Kurt von Hess often used a whip to beat down his opponents.

8. THE HUN

Trained by Kurt von Hess, The Hun pillaged opponents for two decades, beginning in the 1970s. The 280-pound barbarian from Guggenheim was a top draw on the independent circuit.

9. KURT AND KARL VON BRAUNER

Kurt and Karl von Brauner were tag-team champions in the mid-1970s. They infuriated crowds by wearing Nazi uniforms into the ring. The team was managed by Gerhardt Kaiser.

10. FREDERICK VON SCHACHT

Frederick von Schacht wrestled in the years just following World War II. His moniker was one of the most chilling in wrestling history, The Milwaukee Murder Master.

Threats from the East

Like the Germans, Japanese wrestlers were stereotyped following the Second World War. Most of them were devious martial-arts specialists who delighted in punishing American wrestlers. Today, the stereotype is only a memory and wrestling in Japan is extremely popular.

1. ANTONIO INOKI

On June 25, 1976, Antonio Inoki and Muhammad Ali battled to a draw in their wrestler-boxer match. Inoki won the World Wrestling Federation title in November 1979, interrupting Bob Backlund's five-year reign. In 1984, he again proved a giant killer by defeating Hulk Hogan in Japan. Inoki was so popular in Japan that he was elected to their parliament.

2. GIANT BABA

Shohei "Giant" Baba was a big star in professional wrestling for more than thirty years. Nearly seven feet tall and weighing 325 pounds, Giant Baba was a three-time NWA world champion. In 1974, he took the title from Jack Brisco, and he defeated champion Harley Race for the belt in 1979 and

1980. He used judo chops to soften up his opponents and finished them with a size-17 boot to the face.

3. **JUMBO TSURUTA**

Tommy "Jumbo" Tsuruta was trained by The Giant Baba. He put this training to use in defeating Nick Bockwinkel for the AWA world title in February 1984. During his career, Jumbo beat many of professional wrestling's greatest stars, including Ric Flair, Dory Funk, Jr., Terry Funk, Harley Race, and Jack Brisco.

4. **YOKOZUNA**

At over 500 pounds, sumo wrestler Yokozuna proved too much to handle for most wrestlers. Yokozuna wore the WWF world title belt around his ample waist on two occasions in 1993 and 1994. He finished many foes by jumping off the second rope onto their chests.

5. **MASTER SAITO**

Martial-arts expert Master Saito won the WWF tag-team title with Mr. Fuji in 1981 and 1982. Master Saito used both the Japanese stomach claw and the scorpion deathlock as submission holds.

6. **KEIJI MUTO**

Keiji Muto performed in the United States as The Great Muta during the 1990s. The persona was reminiscent of The Great Kabuki. The Great Muta also wore face paint and blew a mysterious mist into opponents' eyes to blind them. A superstar in his homeland, Keiji Muto has held most of the major titles in Japan.

7. **THE GREAT TOGO**

The Great Togo was one of the first Japanese wrestlers to become a headliner in the United States. His feud with fan favorite Antonino Rocca was one of the most heated of the 1950s. His persona of the evil Japanese wrestler was imitated by many who followed.

8. **TOKYO JOE**

Tokyo Joe was a frequent tag-team partner of The Great Togo. His promising career was cut short in 1974 when he lost his right leg and part of his right arm when he was struck by an automobile during a snowstorm near Calgary, Canada.

9. **DR. MOTO**

In 1967, Dr. Moto teamed with Mitsu Arakawa to win the American Wrestling Association world tag-team title. He also wrestled under the name of Tor Kamata.

10. **BULL NAKANO**

The powerful Bull Nakano won the WWF women's title in 1994. The dark-haired rule breaker was the perfect foil for the blonde Alundra Blaze who was a three-time champion during that period.

Cold Warriors

After World War II, The United States engaged in a long Cold War with the Soviet Union. Most of the Russian wrestlers during those years were bad guys who promised to bury their weak American opponents.

1. IVAN KOLOFF

The Russian Bear Ivon Koloff had the reputation of being the most vicious man in wrestling. On January 18, 1971, Koloff achieved the seemingly impossible. He defeated Bruno Sammartino for the WWF world title. The Living Legend had held the title for nearly eight years. In the 1980s, Koloff won NWA world tag-team titles with Ray Stevens, Don Kernodle, and Nikita Koloff.

2. NIKOLAI VOLKOFF

When Nikolai Volkoff entered the World Wrestling Federation in the early 1970s, he appeared to be destined to win championship gold. The 325-pound Russian boasted a chest that measured sixty-five inches. Managed by Fred

Blassie, Volkoff defeated everyone he faced. He destroyed the 400-pound Gorilla Monsoon in a match that lasted only four minutes. Many expected Volkoff to defeat Bruno Sammartino for the WWF title. He and Sammartino wrestled to a fifty-four-minute draw, but Volkoff never could win the title. In 1985, however, he and The Iron Sheik did win the WWF tag-team title.

3.   IVAN AND KAROL KALMIKOFF

Ivan and Karol Kalmikoff were one of professional wrestling's first great tag teams. The Kalmikoffs captured the American Wrestling Association world tag belt in 1961. Ivan later managed several wrestlers, most notably The Mighty Igor.

4.   NIKITA KOLOFF

Nikita Koloff was presented as the "nephew" of Ivan Koloff. He teamed with his "uncle" to win the NWA world tag-team title in 1985. Koloff's real name was Scott Simpson.

5.   BORIS ZHUKOV

Another wrestler who rose to prominence while portraying a Russian was Jim Darrell. As Boris Zhukov, he was an AWA world tag-team champion in 1987 with partner Soldat Ustinov.

6.   BORIS DRAGOFF

Trained by Ivan Koloff, The Russian Hit Man Boris Dragoff made his reputation on the Southern independent circuit in the late 1990s. Dragoff was managed by Count Grog. His finisher was The Russian Guillotine.

7. RUSSIAN ASSASSIN II

The Cold War may have been over, but apparently no one ever told The Russian Assassin II. He still waved the Soviet flag and taunted Americans, occasionally using his chain as a weapon.

8. NIKOLAI ZOLOTOFF

Butcher Vachon is best remembered for teaming up with Mad Dog Vachon. The Vachons were AWA tag-team champions in 1969. Early in his career, Buther Vachon wrestled under the name of Nikolai Zolotoff.

9. IVAN KAMEROFF

Ivan Kameroff was one of the first Russians to become a star in professional wrestling. The Russian Strongman overpowered foes in the NWA during the 1950s.

10. COLONEL NINOTCHKA

Colonel Ninotchka was the wrestler fans most loved to hate in The G.L.O.W. (Gorgeous Ladies of Wrestling) promotion during the late 1980s. Colonel Ninotchka left no doubt about her allegiance to her country. She wore red outfits, red earrings, red nail polish, and red eye shadow. She even had a hammer and sickle painted on her shoulder.

South of the Border

Wrestlers in Mexico often reach the status of cultural heroes. In Mexico, the Lucha Libra (free-fight) style of wrestling emphasizes high-risk aerobatic moves. The masked wrestler is an honored tradition, going back to the ancient Aztec warriors, who wore masks in battle. Here are some of the best wrestlers of Mexican heritage.

1. MIL MASCARAS

Mil Mascaras was an international star whose appeal crossed all boundaries. In 1972, The Man of a Thousand Masks became the first masked wrestler to appear in Madison Square Garden. Madison Square Garden had banned masked athletes from competing there, but the enormous popularity of Mil Mascaras caused them to lift the ban. He didn't let down his fans as he defeated The Spoiler.

2. TITO SANTANA

Tito Santana was one of the most popular and successful Mexican wrestlers of the 1980s. Santana combined technical excellence with aerial skills. The combination helped him win the Intercontinental title in 1984 and again in 1985. Santana also won WWF tag-team titles with Ivan Putski in 1979 and Rick Martel in 1987.

3. EDDY GUERRERO

Eddy Guerrero comes from a wrestling family. His father, Gory, was a star in Mexico. Eddy's brother, Chavo Guerrero, also built a reputation in the United States. While in World Championship Wrestling, Eddy Guerrero won the United States and cruiserweight belts. Once he made the switch to the World Wrestling Federation, it wasn't long before he again wore gold around his waist.

4. CHAVO GUERRERO, JR.

Uncle Eddy proved to be a bad influence on Chavo Guerrero, Jr. When Chavo didn't live up to the Guerrero name, Eddy began making his life miserable. He humiliated Chavo on numerous occasions and interfered in his matches. To add insult to injury, he defeated Chavo in a "hair vs. hair" match. Chavo not only lost his hair, he lost his mind. He underwent more personality changes than Bridey Murphy. Worse yet, he began riding a broomstick horse that he named Pepe.

5. REY MISTERIO, JR.

At 140 pounds, Rey Misterio, Jr. is one of the smallest men ever to enter the squared circle. What he lacks in size, he more than makes up in talent. He earned the nickname "Giant Killer" after improbable victories over Kevin Nash and Bam Bam Bigelow. At last count, he had won the WCW cruiserweight title five times. In October 1999, he and Konnan won the WCW world tag-team belt.

6. JUVENTUD GUERRERA

A star in Mexico's Promo Azteca, Juventud Guerrera is 165 pounds of high-flying fury. He proved he was of championship caliber in America when he won the WCW cruiserweight title in 1998. Guerrera has feuded with Rey Misterio, Jr. throughout the world. One of wrestling's most accomplished aerialists, his signature moves are The 450 Splash and The Juvy Drive.

7. LUIS MARTINEZ

Luis Martinez was a Mexican star during the 1960s and 1970s. The scientific wrestler had many memorable bouts against the sport's worst rule breakers, such as The Sheik and Wild Bull Curry. Martinez joined with Curry's son, Flying Fred Curry, to form a popular tag team.

8. LA PARKA

La Parka won numerous light-heavyweight titles in Mexico. Known as The Man of a Thousand Bones, the wrestler in the skeleton suit is a rare combination of a gifted high-flyer who can also wrestle hardcore matches. His trademark moves are The Corkscrew Moonsault and Tope Suicida. This man truly is bad to the bone.

9. PSICOSIS

Besides owning one of pro wrestling's best names, Psicosis is known for his innovative style. In 1999, he won the WCW cruiserweight title on two separate occasions. He has been involved in prolonged feuds with Rey Misterio, Jr. and La Parka. His tope con hilo is unsurpassed in professional wrestling.

10. **PERRO AGUAYO, SR.**

For thirty years, Perro Aguayo, Sr. has been winning titles in Mexico and also on the independent circuit in the United States. Aguayo is equally adept at scientific wrestling and brawling. He has also wrestled tag team with his son, Perro, Jr.

Cowboys and Cowgirls

The cowboy has become a mythic hero in America. The men, with their ten-gallon hats and fast draws, have been immortalized in films and literature. Since the early years of professional wrestling, the cowboy wrestler has flourished. The Wild West still lives on in the wrestling ring.

1. COWBOY BOB ORTON

A second-generation wrestler, Bob Orton, Jr. was voted the National Wrestling Alliance rookie-of-the-year in 1978. As Cowboy Bob Orton, he became a star. Although Orton was one of wrestling's best technical wrestlers, he often resorted to rulebreaking. As Ace, Roddy Piper's bodyguard, he was one of the WWF's biggest heels in the 1980s. In 1984 he teamed up with Don Kernodle to win the NWA world tag-team belt.

2. COWBOY BOB ELLIS

Bob Ellis was pro wrestling's premier cowboy in the 1950s and 1960s. Cowboy Bob was especially popular in Texas and the Midwest. Ellis and Johnny Valentine won the United

States tag-team championship in 1961. The next year, the duo won the prestigious WWF world tag-team belts.

3. RON BASS

The self-proclaimed "King of the Cowboys," Ron Bass was ornery as a rattlesnake. Attired in cowboy boots and trunks with a double-horseshoe insignia, Bass held several titles during the 1980s, including the Southern heavyweight belt. His roughhouse style and ability to take punishment resulted in many of his matches becoming bloodbaths.

4. COWBOY BOBBY DUNCUM

Rough and tough, Bobby Duncum wore a cowboy hat and boots to the ring. "Big Bad" Bobby was especially effective at tag-team action. Duncum combined with Blackjack Lanza to win the AWA world tag-team title in 1976. The 280-pound Texan is credited with inventing the bulldog headlock, a move inspired by a rodeo technique.

5. THE TEXAS COWGIRLS

Cowgirl Wendi Richter won numerous women's titles in the 1980s. During that decade, she teamed with the powerful Joyce Grable to form The Texas Cowgirls.

6. COWBOY SCOTT HALL

You probably know Scott Hall as one of the leaders of The New World Order. Or you remember him in previous incarnations as the toothpick-chewing Razor Ramon or The Diamond Studd. Few fans recall that Cowboy Scott Hall teamed with Curt Hennig to win the AWA world tag-team belt in 1986.

7. BLACKJACK MULLIGAN

Certainly the biggest cowboy of them all was Blackjack Mulligan. The six-foot nine, 300-pound Texan was one of the few wrestlers who could go toe-to-toe with Andre the Giant.

Mulligan's claw hold ranks with Fritz von Erich's as the most devastating in wrestling history. Mulligan teamed with Bobby Duncum to win the AWA tag-team title in 1976. His favorite tag-team partner was Blackjack Lanza. The Blackjacks wore the WWF tag-team belts in 1975.

8. COWBOY PAT FRALEY

The prototype for the modern cowboy wrestler was Cowboy Pat Fraley. He wrestled throughout the West during the 1950s and 1960s.

9. COWBOY BILL WATTS

Cowboy Bill Watts was a top contender in the National Wrestling Alliance during the 1970s. Watts wore the traditional cowboy wrestler attire: black hat, boots, and a cowhide vest. Watts teamed with Gorilla Monsoon to win the WWF tag belt in 1965.

10. BIG TEX MCKENZIE

Like Bill Watts, Tex McKenzie was a cowboy star of the 1970s. The big Texan also wrestled extensively in Australia and the Far East.

On the Warpath

Professional wrestling has seen a whole tribe of Indian wrestlers over the years.

1. CHIEF WAHOO MCDANIEL

Wahoo McDaniel traced his bloodlines back to the Choctaw-Chippewa tribes. He played professional football for nine seasons before beginning an equally successful career in pro wrestling. McDaniel used his powerful tomahawk chops and Indian deathlock submission hold to win many title belts in the 1980s.

2. CHIEF JAY STRONGBOW

A star for more than thirty years, Chief Jay Strongbow did a war dance before his bouts. Once the bell rang, he softened up foes with knee lifts and tomahawk chops before turning their lights out with his patented Indian Sleeper. His greatest success came as a tag-team wrestler in the World Wrestling Federation. He won world tag-team belts with Sonny King in 1972, Billy Whitewolf in 1976, and twice with Jules Strongbow in 1982.

3. CHIEF DON EAGLE

The Mohawk wrestler Don Eagle was one of the most popular stars during the early days of televised wrestling. The son of wrestler Joseph War Hawk, he won the AWA world championship in 1950.

4. TATANKA

Chris Chavis, otherwise known as Tatanka, was a star in the World Wrestling Federation in the early 1990s. A member of the Lumbee tribe, Tatanka subdued many opponents with his "Papoose to Go" back drops. Originally a babyface, Tatanka turned heel before his departure from the WWF.

5. CHIEF WHITE OWL

Chief White Owl was an outstanding Indian wrestler of the 1960s. Whenever he did a war dance during a match, it was almost always a prelude to victory. A notable exception was a contest against Dick the Bruiser. The Bruiser managed to survive the attack and finish the Chief off with his signature knee drop from the top rope.

6. CHIEF THUNDERBIRD

The first Indian wrestler to wear his ceremonial headdress into the ring, Chief Thunderbird was a sensation throughout the world. The Chief began wrestling during the 1930s.

7. TIGER NELSON

Many wrestlers have posed as Native Americans, but no claim was more outrageous than that of Tiger Nelson. The African-American claimed to be a member of the Blackfoot tribe.

8. CHIEF CHEWCHKI

Another Indian of questionable lineage was Chief Chewchki. During the 1930s, The Chief would pitch a teepee on public land in the town where he was to wrestle that night. When he was confronted by the police, he argued that the land rightfully belonged to the Indians. This ploy garnered publicity for his matches and an occasional night in jail. It was rumored that Chewchki was really a Gypsy.

9. PRINCESS TONA TOMAH

While there were many male Indian wrestlers, Princess Tona Tomah was one of the few Native American women wrestlers. The Chippewa princess was active during the 1950s and 1960s.

10. CHIEF OSLEY SAUNOOKE

Probably the heaviest Indian wrestler was Chief Osley Saunooke. The Cherokee Chief weighed more than 300 pounds and wrestled from the 1930s to the 1950s.

African-American Stars

R on Simmons became the first African-American to win a world title in a major federation. In August 1992, he defeated Vader to win the WCW belt. This list includes ten of the greatest African-American stars in pro wrestling history.

1. THE ROCK

The Rock is probably the most popular and charismatic man in professional wrestling today. If you don't believe it, just ask him. The Rock refers to himself as "The Most Electrifying Man in Sports Entertainment." The self-proclaimed "People's Champion" can back up his boasts. A chip off the old block, he is the son of wrestling great Rocky Johnson. The Rock has held every major title in the World Wrestling Federation. After he drops "The People's Elbow" on his opponents, they find themselves between a Rock and a hard place—the canvas.

2. ROCKY JOHNSON

Although he never reached the superstardom achieved by his son, Rocky Johnson was undeniably one of the premier African-American wrestlers of the 1980s. In 1983, Johnson and Tony Atlas won the World Wrestling Federation tag-team title. His personality was much more low-key than his son's.

3. RON SIMMONS

Before he entered professional wrestling, Ron Simmons was an All-American football player at Florida State. Simmons made wrestling history in 1992 when he won the WCW world heavyweight belt. He became the first African-American to hold a major world title in singles action. When he moved to the World Wrestling Federation, he changed his name to Faarooq. He formed the tag team The Acolytes with partner Bradshaw. The Acolytes won the WWF tag-team title in 1999. Simmons was the former leader of The Nation of Domination.

4. BOBO BRAZIL

The big man from Benton Harbor, Michigan, was pro wrestling's first major black star. The six-foot-six 300-pounder was a top attraction in the 1960s and 1970s. His feud with The Sheik was one of the sport's most heated and prolonged. Brazil used his Koko Headbutt to knock out his opponents. In recognition of his outstanding career, Bobo Brazil was one of the first wrestlers inducted into the World Wrestling Federation Hall of Fame.

5. BOOKER T

Booker T may not have the flair of The Rock, but he quietly amassed one of the best records of the 1990s. Along with his brother Stevie Ray, he formed the tag team known as Harlem Heat. Between 1994 and 1997, Harlem Heat won the WCW tag-team title ten times. Booker T held the WCW television title six times between 1997 and 1999. One of his finishing moves is known as The Harlem Hangover. In July 2000, Booker T defeated Jeff Jarrett to win the WCW world title.

6. STEVIE RAY

Although he had less success as a singles wrestler than his brother, Booker T, Stevie Ray was one-half of the most successful tag team in World Championship Wrestling history. When Booker T was injured, Stevie Ray volunteered to defend his brother's title, which he lost to Chris Jericho in 1998, causing a temporary rift between the brothers. For a time, Stevie Ray became a member of The New World Order black-and-white.

7. TONY ATLAS

The possessor of professional wrestling's best physique, Tony Atlas lived up to his name. Powerful and agile, he was a top contender for tag-team and singles gold during the 1980s. A highlight of his career occurred in 1983 when he and Rocky Johnson won the World Wrestling Federation tag-team title.

8. AHMED JOHNSON

Powerful Ahmed Johnson defeated Goldust at the 1996 *King of the Ring* to win the WWF Intercontinental title. That same year, he won a battle royal to earn a shot at the WWF world heavyweight title, but an injury robbed him of his opportunity. Johnson's finishing move was The Pearl River Plunge.

9. SHAG THOMAS

At five-foot-six and weighing 275 pounds, Shag Thomas was built like a fireplug. He was a popular performer in the

Pacific Northwest during the 1960s. As a singles wrestler, he had numerous feuds with Skull Murphy and The Destroyer. His tag-team partners included Nature Boy Buddy Rogers, Stan Stasiak, and Tough Tony Borne.

10. D-LO BROWN

D-Lo Brown has worked his way up from being a security guard for The Gangstas and a bodyguard for The Nation of Domination to a WWF star. In July 1999, he confirmed his status by winning the prestigious Intercontinental title from future WCW champion Jeff Jarrett. He has held the European title four times. Brown won the belt the first time in 1998 from none other than future WWF world champion Triple-H. Brown's frog-splash, known as The Lo-Down, is one of wrestling's best.

Terrific Tag Teams

Tag-team wrestling has always been an important part of the sport. Wrestlers are usually teamed together because they're related, physically similar, or have complementary styles. These tag specialists stood out from the rest.

1. THE LEGION OF DOOM

"Bashing heads make you feel more alive," said Animal, one-half of the tag team The Legion of Doom. Managed by Paul Ellering, Hawk and Animal bashed heads and left a trail of broken bodies in their path. They won the NWA world title in 1998 and WWF tag belts in 1991 and 1997. Their finisher was The Doomsday Device, a move in which one of them held their opponent while the other clotheslined him from the top rope. In their words, "Oh, what a rush!"

2. THE FABULOUS FREEBIRDS

The Fabulous Freebirds were actually three wrestlers instead of two—Michael Hayes, Terry Gordy, and occasionally Buddy Roberts. The Southern-born stars entered the ring to their theme song, Lynyrd Skynyrd's anthem, "Freebird." Roberts provided the technical skills, Gordy the power, and Hayes the brains and style. Together, they were practically unbeatable. The Freebirds won WCW world tag-team titles in both 1989 and 1991.

3.   THE NASTY BOYS

Brian Knobs and Jerry Sags were The Nasty Boys, a tag team which more than lived up to its name. The Nasty Boys won the WWF world tag-team title in 1991 and held the WCW version on three occasions between 1993 and 1995. They carried on a lengthy feud with Public Enemy.

4.   THE EAST-WEST CONNECTION

Adrian Adonis and Jesse "The Body" Ventura formed a successful tag team known as The East-West Connection. Adonis, from the streets of New York, provided the technical skills, and Ventura, who claimed to be from California, provided the muscle. Adonis and Ventura won the AWA world tag-team title in 1980 and became a top tag team in the World Wrestling Federation in the early 1980s.

5.   THE WILD SAMOANS

The Wild Samoans, Afa and Sika, were one of the most dangerous tag teams of the 1980s. The wildmen wore huge Afros and either beat their opponents senseless or paralyzed them with nerve holds. Managed by the underhanded Captain Lou Albano, The Wild Samoans won WWF world tag-team belts three times between 1980 and 1982.

6.   THE MOONDOGS

The Moondogs may have not been the most technically advanced tag team in wrestling history, but that didn't stop them from being one of the most successful. They did whatever was necessary to win a match, from biting their opponents to hitting them with a bone. In 1981, The Moondogs, Rex and King, won the WWF tag-team title. Later that year, Rex teamed with Spot to recapture the belt. The Moondogs dominated the United States Wrestling Association, winning the tag titles an incredible fourteen times between 1991 and 1996.

7. THE DUDLEY BOYZ

The Dudley Boyz, Buh Buh Ray and D-Von, are the most famous of the Dudley clan to emerge from Dudleyville. In Extreme Championship Wrestling, the Dudleys threw enough opponents through flaming tables to win the tag-team title six times since 1997. Recently, they brought their brand of mayhem to the World Wrestling Federation. The Dudleys won the WWF tag belt in February 2000. Their finishing move is The Dudley Death Drop.

8. THE NATURAL DISASTERS

Earthquake and Typhoon, The Natural Disasters, had a combined weight of nearly 900 pounds. Earthquake, the heavier of the two, enjoyed jumping around a fallen opponent to create seismic activity. Many opponents were squashed by their dreaded double splash. In 1992, The Natural Disasters, managed by Jimmy Hart, won the WWF tag-team belt.

9. THE ROCK AND SOCK CONNECTION

What do The Rock and Mankind have in common? Both have won the WWF world title individually numerous times. Both men have written best-selling books about their wrestling careers. More importantly, they teamed up to form

The Rock and Sock Connection. The Sock part of the name refers to Mr. Socko, the sock which Mankind places on his hand just before he applies his mandible claw. The Rock and Sock Connection won the WWF tag belt three times during 1999.

10. **THE FABULOUS KANGAROOS**

The Fabulous Kangaroos were a premier team in the late 1950s and early 1960s. The duo consisted of Al Costello and Roy Heffernan. The Kangaroos were one of the best synchronized tag teams in the history of wrestling, and they created their own unique style, with original moves such as The Boomerang. The Fabulous Kangaroos won the WWF world tag-team belt in 1960.

Like Father, Like Son

Many professional wrestlers are second-generation stars. Some have even wrestled against their fathers.

1. VERNE AND GREG GAGNE

Verne Gagne, one of the greatest scientific wrestlers, dominated the American Wrestling Association, winning the world heavyweight title nine times between 1960 and 1980. His son, Greg, teamed with Jumping Jim Brunzell to win AWA tag-team titles in 1977 and 1981. Both father and son used the sleeper hold to win matches.

2. DUSTY AND DUSTIN RHODES

The American Dream Dusty Rhodes was a legend in wrestling, winning championship belts throughout the Southern states in the 1970s. His "bionic" elbow made opponents see stars. Rhodes won the NWA world title in 1979, 1981, and 1986. His son, Dustin, achieved only modest success at first. Only after he assumed the bizarre Goldust character did he become a star in his own right. Dustin made fun of his father by imitating him in a less than complimentary way.

3. RIC AND DAVID FLAIR

The Nature Boy Ric Flair has won the NWA/WCW world title a record seventeen times. As he neared the end of his career, he introduced his son, David, to professional wrestling. After a slow start, David Flair won his first world title when he shared the WCW tag-team belt with Crowbar. David soon disavowed his father and conspired against him. David once helped shave his father's head after Ric lost a match.

4. LARRY AND CURT HENNIG

Larry "The Axe" Hennig had the reputation of being one of pro wrestling's toughest men. He was called "The Axe" because of his deadly elbow smash which nearly cut opponents in two. Hennig won AWA world tag-team titles three times between 1965 and 1967 with Harley Race and another time with Duke Hoffman.

During the 1980s, Larry wrestled tag team with his son, Curt. Curt Hennig would eclipse the achievements of his famous father. In 1986, Curt won the AWA tag-team title with Gorgeous Jimmy Garvin. A year later, he defeated Nick Bockwinkel for the AWA world heavyweight title. In the next decade, Hennig added the Intercontinental and United States heavyweight belts to his collection.

5. BLACKJACK MULLIGAN AND BARRY WINDHAM

Blackjack Mulligan was a tough act to follow. He was a top contender in singles action and a tag-team champion with partner Blackjack Lanza. His son, Barry Windham, inherited several things from his father: his height, his toughness, and his affinity for gold. Windham won the WCW tag-team title with Lex Luger in 1988 and later won tag belts with Dustin Rhodes, Curt Hennig, and Kendall Windham. He also won the WWF tag-team title in 1985 with Mike Rotundo.

6. JOHNNY AND GREG VALENTINE

Johnny Valentine slowly and methodically took opponents apart, inflicting injuries and then hammering them until opponents submitted. Johnny won numerous regional singles belts and WWF world tag-team titles with Buddy Rogers, Cowboy Bob Ellis, and Antonio Pugliese.

His son, Greg Valentine, won the WWF Intercontinental title in 1984. The next year, he and Brutus Beefcake became WWF tag-team champs. Valentine was also a two-time United States heavyweight champion. Greg was known as "The Hammer" because of his vaunted elbow smash. Valentine used a figure-four deathlock as his submission hold.

7. WARREN AND NICK BOCKWINKEL

Warren Bockwinkel wrestled from the 1930s to 1950s. Late in his career, he wrestled as a tag team with his son, Nick. The young Bockwinkel went on to stardom in the American Wrestling Association. He combined smooth technical ability with occasional rulebreaking to win his matches. Nick also used his extraordinary verbal skills to antagonize and belittle opponents. He teamed with Ray "The Crippler" Stevens to win AWA world tag-team belts three times. In November 1975, Nick defeated Verne Gagne to capture the AWA world heavyweight title. Managed by Bobby "The Brain" Heenan, he won the world title three more times in the next eleven years.

8.   BRUNO AND DAVID SAMMARTINO

Bruno Sammartino has a record unsurpassed in the annals of the World Wrestling Federation. The Living Legend won the WWF world title in 1963 and held it for nearly eight years. He regained the belt in December 1973 and successfully defended it until 1977. His son, David, also became a professional wrestler, but never approached his father's success.

9.   IVAN AND SCOTT PUTSKI

Polish Power Ivan Putski was one of the strongest men in wrestling. He felled many opponents with his mighty two-handed hammer blow. The WWF star won the world tag-team title with Tito Santana in 1979. His son, Scott, is also a

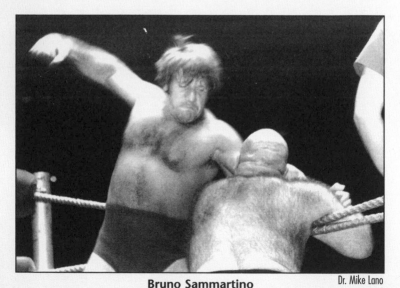

Dr. Mike Lano

Bruno Sammartino

"The Living Legend," Bruno Sammartino, administers a beating to George "The Animal" Steele in a 1974 match.

powerhouse in the ring, but he has yet to duplicate his father's success.

10. JOLTIN' JOE AND TULLY BLANCHARD

Joltin' Joe Blanchard was a popular wrestler in the Midwest and South in the 1960s. His son, Tully, won the United States heavyweight title in 1985. Tully was one of the original Four Horsemen. He and fellow Horseman Arn Anderson were NWA world tag-team champions in 1987 and 1988.

Blood Brothers

In professional wrestling, your brother may or may not be blood kin. For example, The Undertaker and Kane are not real brothers, despite what Paul Bearer might tell you.

1. **TERRY FUNK AND DORY FUNK, JR.**

The Funk brothers have been a force in professional wrestling for more than thirty years. Dory Funk, Jr. reigned as NWA world heavyweight champion from 1963 to 1966 before losing the crown to Harley Race. He regained the title in 1969 and defended it successfully for four more years before once again losing it to Harley Race. His brother, Terry, was the NWA champion from 1974 to 1977 before losing to—you guessed it—Harley Race.

2. **THE GRAHAM BROTHERS**

The Grahams formed a dynasty that dominated professional wrestling from the 1950s to the 1980s. Dr. Jerry Graham teamed up with brother Eddie to win the United States tag-team belts in 1957 and 1959. In 1964 he paired with brother Luke to reclaim the title. Eddie and Jerry also won the WWF world tag-team title three times between 1957 and 1960. Crazy Luke Graham and Jerry won the WWF tag belt in 1964.

Mike Graham was an AWA light-heavyweight champion. By far the most famous of the Grahams was the flamboyant Superstar Billy Graham. He defeated Bruno Sammartino in April 1977 to win the WWF world heavyweight title.

3. JACK AND JERRY BRISCO

The Brisco Brothers were successful both in singles competition and as a tag team. Jack Brisco was a two-time NWA heavyweight champion. The Briscos won the NWA world tag-team titles three times between 1983 and 1984. Their favorite wrestling moves were the sleeper, airplane spin, and figure-four grapevine.

4. RICK AND SCOTT STEINER

The Steiner Brothers were one of the most successful tag teams in professional wrestling history. They first won the WCW world tag-team titles in 1989 and won the belt five more times in the next decade. The team split up when Scott dyed his hair blond and became the heel Big Poppa Pump. For a while, the Steiners were bitter enemies. Scott Steiner launched a successful singles career, winning the U.S. and world titles.

5. BRET AND OWEN HART

Over the past fifteen years, Bret Hart has a stellar record in both tag-team and singles action. As a member of The Hart Foundation, with Jim "The Anvil" Neidhart, Bret won the WCW world tag-team title three times. From 1992 to 1997, he won the WWF world title five times. In 1999, Hart won the WCW world title for the first time.

Younger brother Owen won WWF world tag-team belts with three different partners: Yokozuna (1995), Davey Boy Smith (1996), and Jeff Jarrett (1999). Owen also won the Intercontinental and European titles. The Hart Brothers frequently feuded, with Owen expressing jealousy of his brother's success. In 1994 he declared himself "King of Harts" after winning The King of the Ring Tournament, but lost a cage match to Bret for the WWF championship.

6. RANDY SAVAGE AND LANNY POFFO

Randy Savage is one of the few men ever to win both the World Wrestling Federation and World Championship Wrestling world heavyweight titles. The Macho Man and his brother, Lanny, are the sons of Angelo Poffo, a champion wrestler in the 1960s. Leapin' Lanny Poffo was known for his aerial skills. Poffo's claim to fame was a victory over Hulk Hogan.

7. THE ARMSTRONGS

Brad Armstrong and The Road Dogg are sons of Bob Armstrong, a popular wrestler in his day. Brad's greatest success came at the beginning of his career in the early 1980s. In contrast, The Road Dogg has gotten better with time. As Jesse James Armstrong, Jesse James, The Road Dogg, or as part of The New Age Outlaws, he has worn the WWF world tag-team, the Intercontinental, and WWF hardcore belts.

8. ART AND STAN NEILSON

The Neilson Brothers, Art and Stan, were one of the best tag teams in the early 1960s. The Neilsons won many belts, including the AWA world tag-team title in 1962.

9. JIMMY AND JOHNNY VALIANT

Hailing from the streets of New York City, the Valiant Brothers were two of wrestling's most colorful performers. Handsome Jimmy, also known as The Boogie Woogie Man, alternated between a carefree and maniacal attitude. He teamed with brother Luscious Johnny Valiant to win the WWF world tag-team title in 1974. Five years later, Luscious Johnny teamed with brother Gentleman Jerry Valiant to once again win the WWF tag belt.

10. THE DUDLEYS

The Dudley family claims to be half-brothers. While they bear little physical resemblance to one another, they did all wear glasses which were held together by tape. Big Dick Dudley seems to be the head of the clan. His siblings include D-Von Dudley (who's African-American), Sign Guy Dudley, Chubby Dudley, and the irrepressible Buh Buh Ray Dudley.

Imitation Is the Sincerest Form of Insult

Wrestlers often mock other wrestlers by doing unflattering imitations.

1. CHRIS JERICHO

Chris Jericho has few peers in the art of making fun of opponents. Anything is fair game, from an opponent's appearance to his name. One of Jericho's most memorable mockeries was of Goldberg's entrance to the ring. Goldberg would walk to the ring surrounded by security guards. Jericho walked to the ring with an overweight guard named Ralphus who led him through wrong doors, into closets, and finally through an exit door. Jericho found himself locked outside the arena.

2. YVAN THE IMITATOR

Wrestling's top impressionist, Yvan the Imitator has won titles on the Northern independent circuit. He has done scathing impressions of WWF stars Gangrel and Goldust, as well as opponents such as Frankie the Mobster.

3. THE nACHO MAN AND THE HUCKSTER

When two of his biggest stars, Hulk Hogan and Randy "Macho Man" Savage, left the World Wrestling Federation for rival World Championship Wrestling, WWF owner Vince McMahon decided to get even. He ran tapes of two scrawny old men imitating Savage and Hogan. The Macho Man became the Nacho Man and the Hulkster became the Huckster. The two made pathetic attempts to wrestle, wheezing and faking heart attacks. McMahon also poked fun at WCW owner Ted Turner, who was depicted as bumbling owner Billionaire Ted.

4. DEGEnERATIOn X

Degeneration X were the bad boys of the World Wrestling Federation in the late 1990s. One of Degeneration X's best routines was a comic send-up of a rival wrestling group, The Nation of Domination. Hunter Hearst Helmsley did a hilarious imitation of The Rock, whom he called The Crock. X-Pac mocked strongman Mark Henry by doing a Fat Albert imitation. Others involved in the parody included The Road Dogg as D-Lo Brown and Billy Gunn as The Godfather.

5. THE nEW WORLD ORDER

Another devastating group parody took place in World Championship Wrestling. Members of The New World Order, led by Kevin Nash, ridiculed The Four Horsemen. Nash did a brutal imitation of Arn Anderson, who had recently announced his retirement from the Horsemen. His makeup was less than flattering, and Nash repeatedly made fun of Anderson's age. He made light of Anderson's offer to relinquish his spot as a Horsemen. "You can have my spot, not my liver spot, not my dog Spot..." Syxx skewered The Nature Boy Ric Flair by wearing a white fright wig and a ridiculous putty nose.

6. JASON SENSATION

In the 1990s, Jason Sensation occasionally appeared on WWF broadcasts to do on-the-mark imitations of wrestlers. Those who were given the needle included The Undertaker and Jeff Jarrett. Without question, Sensation's best imitation was of The Rocket Owen Hart, complete with a false hooked nose.

7. THE BLUE MEANIE

One of wrestling's best mimics, The Blue Meanie loved to poke fun at WWF and WCW stars. He started a feud with Goldust by doing an imitation that he called Bluedust. He transformed The New World Order into The Blue World Order.

8. THE NEW RAZOR RAMON AND NEW DIESEL

Promoter Vince McMahon did a lousy job of replacing Diesel and Razor Ramon when Kevin Nash and Scott Hall left his WWF for the WCW. The New Diesel and The New Razor Ramon lasted about as long as New Coke.

9. NWO STING

The New World Order liked to play mind games with wrestlers from the WCW. One of their tricks was to have a wrestler dressed as Sting turn against WCW wrestlers. For a time it appeared that the WCW's most loyal wrestler had defected to the rival NWO. Sting finally stepped forward to discredit the impostor.

10. **POSITIVELY KANYON**

In 2000, Kanyon turned against his old friend, Diamond Dallas Page. As Positively Kanyon, he mocked everything about Page, from his hair to his voice. He made fun of DDP's book, *Positively Page,* by staging a book signing at which nobody came. He even used Page's signature move, The Diamond Cutter, on Buff Bagwell's mother.

It's Humiliating

It's not enough for some wrestlers to defeat an opponent. They have to humiliate them.

1. PAT PATTERSON

Rikishi Phatu, the 420-pound Samoan, humiliates his opponents with his notorious Stink Face move, in which he rubs his ample rear in their faces. He got his comeuppance in May 2000 when Pat Patterson, the former Intercontinental champion, rubbed his butt in Rikishi's face. The joke backfired when Patterson pulled down his pants and fans were able to see a large brown stain on his shorts.

2. VAL VENIS

Self-proclaimed porn star Val Venis humiliated his enemies in a very personal way. Venis showed tapes on the Titan Tron of himself in bed with the wives and loved ones of his opponents. The women seen in compromising positions included Terri, wife of Dustin Runnels, and Ken Shamrock's sister.

3. CHYNA

Mark Henry developed a crush on Chyna. While Chyna rebuffed the advances of Sexual Chocolate, she did suggest that her friend, Sammy, might be interested in him. The budding romance came to an abrupt end when Henry discovered that Sammy was really a man.

4. THE BIG BOSS MAN

The Big Boss Man has a real mean streak. He ground up Al Snow's pet dog and fed Al the beloved pooch. When The Big Show's father passed away, The Big Boss Man dragged his coffin behind his car.

5. KEVIN NASH

Political incorrectness may have reached a new low at the In Your House pay-per-view when Kevin Nash tore off the prosthetic leg of retired wrestling great Mad Dog Vachon.

6. PERRY SATURN

At the Souled Out '99 pay-per-view, Perry Saturn lost a match. A stipulation of the match was that the loser had to wear a dress for 90 days. Saturn honored his commitment and wrestled in a dress. What bothered fans was that he began to like his new wrestling attire.

7. ROWDY RODDY PIPER

Being interviewed on *Piper's Pit* often turned into a humiliating experience. Host Roddy Piper saved his best barbs for Superfly Jimmy Snuka. The Superfly hailed from the Fiji Islands, so Piper tried to make him feel at home by presenting him with a bag of tropical fruit. When Snuka didn't properly express his appreciation for the gift, Piper hit him over the head with a coconut and proceeded to rub a banana into his face. The humiliation initiated one of pro wrestling's most intense feuds.

8. THE DESTROYER

In November 1962, Gorgeous George agreed to a match against the masked Destroyer. If George lost, his head would be shaved. If he won, the Destroyer would have to remove his mask and reveal his identity. The Destroyer won the match and Gorgeous George's blond, curly locks were history.

9. THE 1-2-3 KID

A low point in the career of The 1-2-3 Kid occurred in 1996. After losing a crybaby match to Razor Ramon, The Kid was forced to wear a diaper.

10. DIESEL

The worst kind of humiliation is suffering a quick defeat. At the end of his career, Nature Boy Buddy Rogers was twice defeated in less than a minute by Bruno Sammartino. In November 1994, Diesel challenged Bob Backlund for his World Wrestling Federation championship belt. Diesel destroyed the three-time world champion in a match which lasted only six seconds.

Adding Insult to Injury

During any wrestling telecast, as much time is spent talking as wrestling. Wrestlers use this time to threaten their opponents, and a wrestler with superior verbal skills will usually become a star, even if his wrestling technique is not the best.

1. **ROWDY RODDY PIPER**

The King of the Put Down Artists, Rowdy Roddy Piper rarely loses a match or a verbal exchange. When debating whether to hit a woman, Piper declared himself an "equal opportunist." The unpredictable one described his philosophy when he said, "Just when they think they have all the answers, I change the questions."

2. **JESSE "THE BODY" VENTURA**

Jesse "The Body" Ventura was another whose verbal dexterity equaled his wrestling prowess. He was an obvious choice to become an announcer once his wrestling career was over. When B. Brian Blair, a member of the tag team known as The Killer Bees, was eliminated during a battle royal, Ventura quipped, "Back to the hive!" He called lantern-jawed Sgt. Slaughter "Jarhead." Whenever possible, Ventura extolled his own many virtues. "When you're as great as I am, success comes naturally," The Body declared.

3. JERRY "THE KING" LAWLER

As a wrestler, Jerry "The King" Lawler won the AWA world title and was USWA champion twenty-six times. The King may be an even better commentator than he was a wrestler. The quick-witted Lawler is especially good with risqué material. About Terri Runnels' breasts he once observed, "They make a lovely couple." Lawler was also the man who dubbed Debra McMichaels' breasts "puppies."

4. BOBBY "THE BRAIN" HEENAN

Bobby "The Brain" Heenan was a good wrestler and a great manager, but he's an even better commentator. Heenan proudly refers to his position as "broadcast journalist." He loves to insult wrestling fans, whom he calls "humanoids." However, his favorite targets are the wrestlers, usually babyfaces he doesn't like. He once said, "I have more tricks up my sleeve than The Bushwackers have fleas."

5. GORILLA MONSOON

Heenan's broadcast partner for many years in the World Wrestling Federation was Gorilla Monsoon. Gorilla was known for his advanced vocabulary and extensive knowledge of the human body that he displayed while describing wrestling holds. He popularized the catchphrase, "Stick a fork in him—he's done."

6. THE ROCK

No one can work a crowd into a frenzy faster than The Rock. He has created a series of catchphrases familiar to WWF fans. His most famous utterance is "Smell what The Rock is cooking." He promises to "lay the smack down" on all the "jabronies" who face him in the ring.

7. STONE COLD STEVE AUSTIN

Among wrestlers who excel at inciting crowds, The Rock's top rival is Stone Cold Steve Austin. He tells his fans that he's about to "break out a can of whoop ass," and he usually delivers. His version of the Scriptures, Austin 3:16, reads, "I just kicked your ass."

8. NICK BOCKWINKEL

The most articulate of wrestlers, Nick Bockwinkel was a four-time AWA world champion. A heel for most of his career, he prided himself for his subtle rulebreaking. His verbal barbs were also restrained. He claims that he never lost a verbal bout, and he's probably right.

9. CHRIS JERICHO

Of all the young wrestlers, Chris Jericho is the most skilled verbally. He is intent on adding to his legion of fans, whom he refers to as the "Jericholics." The "Ayatollah of Rock 'n' Rolla" is sure to find an opponent's weak spot and verbally attack it, whether it be Chyna's femininity or an opponent's name, such as calling Dean Malenko "Stinko."

10. **THE GENIUS**

In the early 1990s, Leapin' Lanny Poffo was known to WWF audiences as The Genius, the world's smartest man. Dressed in a cap and gown, he read poems that ridiculed other wrestlers.

Small Packages

In a world populated with 300-pound wrestlers, there is still room for the little man. All of the following wrestlers weigh less than 200 pounds.

1. REY MISTERIO, JR.

Only five-foot three and 140 pounds, Rey Misterio, Jr. earned the nickname "The Giant Killer" because of his victories over two of the giants of the ring, Bam-Bam Bigelow and Kevin Nash. Misterio also dominated wrestlers his size and has won the WCW cruiserweight belt five times.

2. LITTLE SPIKE DUDLEY

Another giant killer, Spike Dudley also holds victories over Bam-Bam Bigelow and The One Man Gang. The 155-pounder has been known to jump out of balconies onto opponents. Spike calls his finishing move The Acid Drop.

3. BLITZKRIEG

With a name like Blitzkrieg, you wouldn't expect a 160-pound wrestler. His name may infer a tank attack, but Blitzkrieg does most of his damage with aerial maneuvers such as his finishing move, a 450 corkscrew splash.

4. ULTIMO DRAGON

The Ultimo Dragon is pound-for-pound one of the most talented wrestlers in the world. He has won both the WWF light-heavyweight title and the WCW cruiserweight belt. He softens up his opponents with moonsaults and other high-flying moves, then finishes them off with his Dragon Sleeper.

5. BATTLE MONKEY

The man with the furry simian mask, Battle Monkey used aerial tactics to defeat larger men. The only way to control him was to play loud rap music.

6. HEAVY METAL

Despite his name, Heavy Metal is a lightweight. The heavy-metal maniac has won numerous titles in Mexico. Popular on the independent circuit, he frequently teamed with The Latin Lover.

7. MIKEY WHIPWRECK

Mikey Whipwreck became the first wrestler to win the ECW world heavyweight, tag-team, and TV titles. He twice won the ECW tag belt with partner Cactus Jack, but has also wrestled tag team with another giant killer, Spike Dudley.

8. **SHINJIRO OTANI**

Japanese star Shinjiro Otani uses an incredible assortment of aerial moves, including The Swan Dive DDT and springboard dropkick. He relies on The Dragon Suplex as his finisher.

9. **RECKLESS YOUTH**

Reckless Youth has earned the nickname "The King of the Independents." His vast repertoire of moves is comparable to wrestlers in any weight division. He uses The Stretch Plum as his submission hold.

10. **EL GRAN HAMADA**

Only five feet, four inches tall and weighing less than 200 pounds, El Gran Hamada has been a top junior heavyweight wrestler around the world for more than twenty years. His signature moves include the windup headbutt and swinging DDT.

Heavies

On the other end of the scale are wrestling's super heavyweights. These wrestlers weigh more than many tag teams.

1. THE McGUIRE TWINS

Wrestling the McGuire Twins, Billy and Benny, was like facing two Jumbo 727s. Each brother tipped (or broke) the scales at 727 pounds.

2. HAPPY HUMPHERY

Happy Humphery may have been the heaviest wrestler ever to step in the ring. Although his normal wrestling weight was around 620 pounds, it was believed that he once ballooned to more than 800 pounds. Humphery's heyday was the 1960s.

3. HAYSTACKS CALHOUN

Haystacks Calhoun liked to list his weight at 601 pounds, apparently to separate him from any mere 600-pounders. Dressed in overalls and wrestling barefoot, Haystacks teamed with Tony Garea to win the WWF tag-team title in 1973. Calhoun finished off his opponents with the dreaded Big Splash. "There's going to be a lot of human pancakes around here before I get finished," he boasted.

4. YOKOZUNA

Yokozuna's weight fluctuated between 570 and 600 pounds. The huge sumo wrestler held the WWF world heavyweight title in 1993 and 1994.

5. FRANK FINNEGAN

One of the heaviest wrestlers of the 1990s, Frank Finnegan weighed nearly 600 pounds. The former WWA champion defeated the better-known big man King Kong Bundy. Finnegan was trained by Tricky Nicky.

6. GATOR

The 525-pound Gator teamed with Country Boy Chris to form the tag team The Giant Hillbillies. His version of the big splash was called The Gator Bomb.

7. THE RASTA SAVAGE

One of the things that's bigger in Texas is The Rasta Savage. At 525 pounds, the Jamaican won championship belts in Texas during the 1990s.

8. MABEL

As Mabel, he won the 1995 WWF King of the Ring Tournament. The six-foot-ten, 500-pound wrestler was one-half of the tag team Men on a Mission, which held the WWF world tag-team belt in 1994. His character took a strange turn in the late 1990s when he returned to the WWF as Viscera, a member of The Corporate Ministry.

9. CHRIS TAYLOR

The former Iowa State wrestling star won a bronze medal in the super-heavyweight division at the 1972 Olympics. He used his superior wrestling technique and 450-pound frame to become a pro wrestling star in the 1970s.

10. KING KONG BUNDY

During a match in New York with Primo Carnera III, King Kong Bundy broke the ring with his tremendous girth. After his big splash knocked the wind out of an opponent, Bundy would arrogantly ask the referee to count to five instead of three.

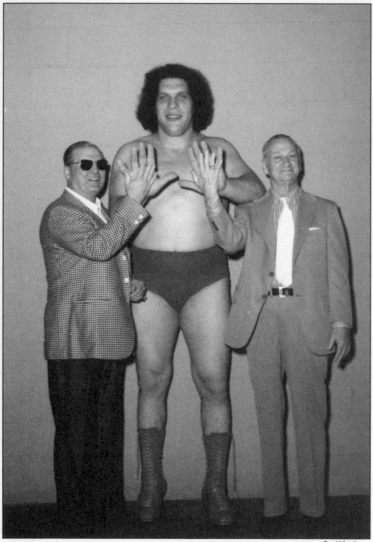

Andre the Giant

Andre the Giant, pictured here with event promoters, was truly a larger-than-life figure in professional wrestling. His booming voice, massive frame, and ability to bludgeon opponents into submission made him one of wrestling's all-time greats.

Giants

Hulk Hogan is a huge man at six-foot-seven, but he'd have to look up to stare eye-to-eye with any of the following wrestlers.

1. THE GIANT GONZALEZ

Believe it or not, Andre the Giant was not the tallest man in pro wrestling history. El Gigante was reported to be seven feet, seven inches tall. However, he was not particularly muscular by wrestling standards. During his stay in the WWF as The Giant Gonzalez, he wrestled in a ridiculous padded bodysuit which had muscles drawn on it.

2. ANDRE THE GIANT

At seven feet, five inches tall and weighing 520 pounds, Andre the Giant was truly "The Eighth Wonder of the World." A wrestling legend, he was literally the biggest attraction in the sport during his career. His feats of eating and drinking are part of wrestling lore. Andre once drank 117 beers at one sitting.

3. THE BIG SHOW

Paul Wight is so big that he was originally billed as the son of Andre the Giant. At seven feet, four inches and nearly 500 pounds, Wight is almost as large as Andre and much more mobile. In 1996, The Giant, as he was known in WCW, won the world heavyweight belt. He changed his name to The Big Show when he defected to the WWF. In 1999, he defeated Triple H to win the WWF world heavyweight title.

4. KEVIN NASH

Seven-foot Kevin Nash played basketball for the University of Tennessee. "Big Sexy" won the WWF world title as Diesel in 1994 and the WCW world championship as Kevin Nash in 1998. His Powerbomb, in which Nash lifts his opponent onto his shoulders and hurls him to the mat, is so dangerous that it has been banned at times.

5. KURRGAN

Almost seven feet tall and 350 pounds, Kurrgan stood out as a member of the group of misfits known in the WWF as The Oddities. A claim to fame is that he was once managed by Sable.

6. THE GIANT BABA

Japanese wrestlers are not normally known for their height, but The Giant Baba was an exception. The six-foot, ten-inch giant won more titles than any wrestler in the history of Japanese wrestling, and in the U.S., held the National Wrestling Alliance world title three times.

7. THE WALL

The Wall, a six-foot, ten-inch powerhouse, was originally brought to WCW as a bodyguard for Berlyn. He quickly out-grew his employer and became a wrestler. Almost impossible to hurt, he became an enforcer in the WCW.

8. BIG JOHN STUDD

Big John Studd lived up to his name. The six-foot, nine-inch, 365-pounder claimed he was the true giant of wrestling. This prompted a prolonged feud with Andre the Giant.

9. SID VICIOUS

During his career, he has been known as Sid Justice, Sycho Sid, and Sid Vicious. By whatever name he goes by, this six-foot, nine-inch terror has power-bombed many wrestlers into oblivion. He and Dan Spivey once formed the tag team known as The Skyscrapers. The vicious one has won both the WWF and WCW world heavyweight titles.

10. VAN HAMMER

The six-foot, eight-inch, 320-pound Van Hammer has always seemed a wrestler in search of a gimmick. He has been everything from a hippie to a member of Raven's Flock.

Total Packages

Wrestlers are better conditioned than they used to be. Long hours in the gym have resulted in some incredible physiques. These men could really flex their muscles.

1. TONY ATLAS

Few, if any, wrestlers could match the physique of Tony Atlas. The former Mr. USA bodybuilding champion was a champion in the wrestling ring as well. Atlas was a WCW tag-team champion in 1983.

2. LEX LUGER

Lex Luger has been called "The Man with a Million Dollar Body." When Luger joined the WWF in 1992, he was selected to be the spokesperson for the new World Bodybuilding Federation. Billed as The Narcissist in the WWF, he brought a mirror into the ring and posed in front of it before each match. He proved he really was "The Total Package" by winning the WCW world title in 1991 and 1997.

3. **SUPERSTAR BILLY GRAHAM**

Billy Graham won many bodybuilding titles, including Mr. Teenage America. His twenty-three inch "guns" were voted "best arms" at the 1976 Pro Mr. America contest. Graham was justifiably proud of his fifty-six-inch chest. Superstar Billy defeated Bruno Sammartino in 1977 to win the WWF title. Graham later admitted he had abused steroids and suffered many health problems as a result.

4. **HULK HOGAN**

No one had ever seen anyone like Hulk Hogan. Nearly six feet, eight inches tall and weighing over 300 pounds, Hogan possessed a magnificent physique for such a huge man. He boasted about his twenty-four-inch "Pythons." Hulk Hogan won the WWF title a record five times and became the most popular wrestler in the history of the sport. He survived a steroid scandal to win the WCW world title six times.

5. **BIG POPPA PUMP**

Big Poppa Pump, better known as Scott Steiner, has twenty-five-inch arms, even bigger than Hogan's legendary Pythons. A six-time WWF world tag-team champion with his brother, Rick, Steiner has also held the United States title.

6. **BUFF BAGWELL**

When he isn't posing to show off his fantastic physique, Marcus "Buff" Bagwell is one of the top stars in WCW. In 1993, Bagwell won the WCW tag-team title with partner Too Cold Scorpion. Two years later he regained the title as part of The American Males with partner Scotty Riggs. He was also the delicious half of the Vicious and Delicious tag team with Scott Norton. Buff truly does have the stuff.

Hulk Hogan

Dr. Mike Lano

Hulk Hogan uses his twenty-four-inch "pythons" to manhandle Lex Luger outside the ring.

7. JESSE "THE BODY" VENTURA

Jesse Ventura was convinced that he possessed the perfect body. "I have the most beautiful body in professional wrestling," he modestly proclaimed. He flexed his muscles at every opportunity. "I'm the master poser," he said. The Body modeled his character after his hero, Superstar Billy Graham.

8. THE PROTOTYPE

The Prototype, a young blond wrestler, has been winning regional titles in the West. With his incredible physique and no-nonsense attitude, it's just a matter of time until he makes his mark in the major federations.

9. KERRY VON ERICH

Kerry von Erich had one of the most perfect physiques in wrestling history. Powerful yet agile, he won the NWA world title in 1984 from Ric Flair and the Intercontinental title in 1990.

10. NATURE BOY BUDDY ROGERS

In the era before steroids and bodybuilding, Nature Boy Buddy Rogers had the ideal wrestling physique. Rogers won both the NWA and WWF world titles.

Wrestler's Wrestlers

They used to call them scientific wrestlers. Now they're known as technicians. Not all wrestling champions have great wrestling ability. Showmanship has made the technician an endangered species. These men could really wrestle.

1. LOU THESZ

Lou Thesz was known as "The Greatest Wrestler in the World" for a good reason. Between 1937 and 1961, Thesz won the National Wrestling Alliance world championship five times. He was taught to wrestle by his father, himself a Greco-Roman wrestler. Due to his incredible wrestling skill, he consistently defeated younger and larger wrestlers.

2. AL COSTELLO

The original "Man of a Thousand Holds," Al Costello not only mastered existing holds, he invented a few himself. A skilled singles wrestler, his greatest fame came as part of the world champion tag team The Fabulous Kangaroos. He prided himself on his wrestling ability and had contempt for less-skilled wrestlers. Prior to a match with Wild Bull Curry, Costello cracked, "He doesn't know a wristlock from a wristwatch."

3. DEAN MALENKO

Dean Malenko is a throwback to days when wrestling ability was more important than showmanship. Also known as "The Man of a Thousand Holds," Malenko learned most of them from his father, ex-wrestler Professor Boris Malenko. In 1999, Dean teamed with The Canadian Crippler Chris Benoit to win the 1999 WCW world tag-team title.

4. COWBOY BOB ORTON

Cowboy Bob Orton was another second-generation wrestler. His father was "The Big O" Bob Orton, a wrestling star of the 1950s. Although he was a heel most of his career, Bob Orton Jr. was one of the best technical wrestlers of his generation. His wrestling moves, such as his drop kick, were textbook.

5. BILLY ROBINSON

Billy Robinson has been called "The Wrestler's Wrestler." An international star, Robinson introduced many European-style holds into American wrestling. It was said that during his matches, other wrestlers would come out of the dressing room to watch—the ultimate compliment. His fluid combinations of moves were unsurpassed.

6. **BRET HART**

According to Bret Hart, he's "the best there is, the best there was, and the best there ever will be." He backed up his boast by winning the WWF title five times. Hart continually pointed out his technical skill, dubbing himself "The Excellence of Execution." His finishing hold was the Sharpshooter, his version of the Boston Crab.

7. **VERNE GAGNE**

Verne Gagne was an amateur wrestling champion, winning the NCAA championship in 1949. One of the great scientific wrestlers in pro-wrestling history, Gagne was a nine-time AWA world champion. He helped teach a future generation of wrestling stars, with his protégés including Ric Flair and Bob Backlund.

8. **BOB BACKLUND**

Bob Backlund was the NCAA wrestling champion in 1971. His mastery of Greco-Roman wrestling quickly earned him a reputation as a superior mat technician as a professional. He won the WWF world title from Superstar Billy Graham in 1978 and held it for five years.

9. **DANNY HODGE**

Danny Hodge was an outstanding amateur wrestler and boxer. He was a NCAA wrestling champion and won a silver medal at the 1956 Olympics. As a professional, he dominated the junior heavyweight division for more than a decade until a horrific automobile accident ended his career.

10. **BRAD RHEINGANS**

An NCAA wrestling champion, Brad Rheingans narrowly missed winning a medal at the 1976 Olympics. As a professional, he was considered one of the best technical wrestlers of the 1980s. His arsenal included a number of suplexes. In 1989, he teamed with Ken Patera to win the AWA world tag-team title.

High Flyers

Some of the most exciting wrestlers are the high flyers. These men defy gravity with their high-risk aerial moves.

1. **SUPERFLY JIMMY SNUKA**

Superfly Jimmy Snuka inspired a whole generation of wrestlers with his spectacular aerial skills. His signature move was a frog splash from the top rope, in which he would jump onto his prone opponent in the center of the ring. In a 1982 match for the WWF world title against champion Bob Backlund, Superfly leaped from the top of a fifteen-foot cage. Backlund moved out of the way and retained his title. Legendary wrestler Lou Thesz called Snuka the greatest showman in wrestling. Snuka teamed with Ray "The Crippler" Stevens to win the NWA world tag-team title in 1980 and was the first ECW heavyweight champion in 1992.

2. **EDOUARD CARPENTIER**

A former acrobat, French wrestler Edouard Carpentier performed amazing aerial maneuvers. One of his favorite moves was a series of front flips onto his opponent. The Flying Frenchman defeated Lou Thesz to win the AWA world title in 1957 and held the belt for more than a year.

3. ANTONINO ROCCA

One of the most popular wrestlers in the early days of televised wrestling, Antonino "Argentina" Rocca was a master of the drop kick. A fitness fanatic, Rocca did two hundred push-ups before each match. He loved to get an opponent in a flying headscissors and ride on his shoulders. His submission hold was The Argentine Backbreaker.

4. JUMPING JIM BRUNZELL

Jumping Jim Brunzell used his extraordinary leaping ability to become one of the top tag-team wrestlers of the 1970s and 1980s. He and Greg Gagne formed the tag team known as The High Flyers. They won AWA world tag-team titles in 1977 and 1981.

5. GREG GAGNE

The other half of The High Flyers, Greg Gagne had one of the best drop kicks in the business. The son of wrestling legend Verne Gagne, Greg achieved tremendous height in his flying knee drops.

6. FLYING FRED CURRY

Fred Curry was the son of Wild Bull Curry, but he inherited none of his father's rule-breaking style. A pure scientific wrestler, he earned his nickname "Flying Fred" due to his high-flying style. Curry was extremely popular on the Mid-western circuit in the 1960s.

7. FLYIN' BRIAN PILLMAN

A former professional football player with the Cincinnati Bengals, Flyin' Brian Pillman was one of wrestling's best aerial artists until he broke an ankle in an automobile accident. In 1993, Pillman and Steve Austin, known as The Hollywood Blonds, won the WCW world tag-team title. Pillman was known as "The Loose Cannon" because of his unpredictable behavior.

8. SABU

Most high flyers are scientific wrestlers, but Sabu is an exception. Sabu combines his aerial skills with a hardcore mentality. He is willing to sacrifice his body if it means injuring a foe. His repertoire includes corkscrew twists, backward flips, somersaults, and swan dives onto unfortunate opponents. Frequently banned for his dangerous tactics, Sabu won the ECW world title in 1993 and 1997.

9. LEAPIN' LANNY POFFO

His brother, Randy Savage, has won many titles with his famed flying elbow drop, but Leapin' Lanny Poffo was the best aerialist in the family. Leapin' Lanny never approached the success of his brother, but he did display his high-flying skills in the WWF during the early 1990s, before turning to managing.

10. MARVIN MERCER

Few fans have ever heard of Marvin Mercer, an acrobatic wrestler of the 1950s. Mercer perfected a move that he called "The Atomic Dropkick," in which he drop kicked an opponent and somehow managed to land on his feet.

They Never Won a World Title

Worcom world titles in professional wrestling seem to change hands every week. Most superstars have been world champions multiple times. This hasn't always been the case. In the old days, world champions frequently held their belts for years. Believe it or not, these wrestling superstars have never won the WWF or WCW world heavyweight title.

1. **ROWDY RODDY PIPER**

Roddy Piper is a wrestling legend, a main-eventer for twenty years. He was Hulk Hogan's nemesis during The Hulkster's heyday and wrestled in the main event of the first Wrestlemania. The rowdy Scot has held both the United States and Intercontinental titles. The one belt he has never worn is the world heavyweight title belt.

2. **SUPERFLY JIMMY SNUKA**

Another wrestling icon, Superfly Jimmy Snuka has done it all in professional wrestling. He's been a world tag-team champion and an ECW world heavyweight champion. The only thing missing from his resume is a WCW or WWF world heavyweight title.

3. GORGEOUS GEORGE

Gorgeous George may be the most famous wrestler in the sport's history. He brought showmanship to professional wrestling. Many people bought their first television set in hopes of seeing the vain and arrogant wrestler get beat. He was featured on the small screen so often in those days that, like Milton Berle, he was called "Mr. Television." Despite his notoriety, Gorgeous George never won the National Wrestling Alliance world title, the most prestigious belt of the time. He did briefly hold the American Wrestling Association world championship title in the early 1950s.

4. THE SHEIK

The Sheik lost so few matches during the 1960s and 1970s that it was said attendance eventually dropped because of the outcome's predictability. The wildman from Syria won the United States title many times, but the major world titles always eluded him.

5. FRED BLASSIE

Fred Blassie's flamboyant style and bad-to-the-bone attitude made him stand out from most other wrestlers in the 1950s and 1960s. Muhammad Ali acknowledged that he had learned showmanship by watching Blassie and Gorgeous George on television. Comedian Andy Kaufman considered Blassie a mentor. In the early 1960s, Blassie won a version of the world title from Edouard Carpentier, but he never held the WWF or NWA championship belts.

6. KILLER KOWALSKI

Killer Kowalski was one of the men who helped popularize professional wrestling. Perhaps the most-hated man in wrestling during the 1950s, he wrestled all over the world. Although Kowalski won many title belts during his long career, he was never recognized as a world champion.

7. BOBO BRAZIL

Bobo Brazil was a top African-American wrestling star in the 1960s. At six-foot-six and 300 pounds, he was a giant in his day. Brazil won the United States title many times, but never a world title. It would be another thirty years before an African-American wrestler, Ron Simmons, would win a world title.

8. KING KONG BUNDY

King Kong Bundy was a 450-pound wrecking machine. He defeated opponents so convincingly that he demanded that the referee count to five instead of three. Bundy wrestled for the title many times but never left the ring as a world champion.

9. GREG VALENTINE

Greg "The Hammer" Valentine was a star in both the NWA and WWF in the 1980s. He won both the Intercontinental and United States titles. Valentine once beat WWF champion Hulk Hogan to a bloody pulp but was unable to wrest away Hogan's title belt.

10. **STAN HANSEN**

Nobody was rougher and tougher than the big Texan Stan Hansen. The 325-pounder had the reputation as pro wrestling's number-one bounty hunter. Whenever someone wanted a wrestler injured, Hansen got the call. He broke champion Bruno Sammartino's neck but could not win his WWF belt. In 1985, Hansen did win the AWA version of the world championship.

Unlikely Champions

In recent years professional wrestling has labeled itself as sports entertainment. The storylines have become more outlandish. Retired wrestlers, women, wrestling executives, and even non-wrestlers have won major championship belts.

1. DAVID ARQUETTE

Actor David Arquette starred in the wrestling movie *Ready to Rumble*. The film featured wrestlers from World Championship Wrestling. Arquette appeared on WCW broadcasts to promote the movie. In April 2000, WCW world champion Jeff Jarrett agreed to put his title on the line in a tag-team match. Jarrett and Eric Bischoff were pitted against Diamond Dallas Page and David Arquette. Although he had never wrestled professionally, Arquette pinned Bischoff to become the most unlikely WCW world champion in history.

2. **VINCE MCMAHON**

World Wrestling Federation owner Vince McMahon was over fifty years old when he began wrestling. In great shape for a man his age, he was involved in several matches and feuded with the WWF's biggest star, Stone Cold Steve Austin. In September 1999, McMahon achieved the unthinkable by winning the WWF world title.

3. **SHANE MCMAHON**

Months before Vince McMahon won the WWF world title, his son, Shane, was already a champion. In February 1999, Shane won the European title. Although a novice at professional wrestling, Shane McMahon wasn't afraid to perform high-risk moves. He proclaimed himself The Giant Killer after defeating the 500-pound Big Show.

4. **STEPHANIE MCMAHON**

In 2000, Stephanie McMahon became the latest member of her family to wear championship gold around her waist. The daughter of Vince, she needed outside interference from X-Pac to win the WWF women's title from Jacqueline.

5. **ERIC BISCHOFF**

Ted Turner owns World Championship Wrestling, but Eric Bischoff was the man often calling the shots. Undersized and inexperienced as a professional wrestler, Bischoff surprised everybody by winning the WCW hardcore title in June 2000. What made it even more unbelievable was that he defeated hardcore icon Terry Funk.

6. **DAFFNEY**

Daffney can best be described as an insane pig-tailed doll. Her constant screeching has unnerved fans and opponents alike. She shocked everyone in 2000 by becoming the first woman to win the WCW cruiserweight championship.

7. **JERRY BRISCO**

Jerry Brisco was a tag-team champion in the early 1980s with his brother, Jack. For the last several years, Brisco has been an official with the World Wrestling Federation. The ex-wrestler turned back the clock by winning the WWF hard-core title in 2000.

8. **PAT PATTERSON**

Like Jerry Brisco, Pat Patterson was a former wrestler who became an executive with the World Wrestling Federation. When Jerry Brisco regained the hardcore title, Patterson threw a party for his friend. During the celebration, Patterson smashed a champagne bottle over Brisco's head. According to hardcore rules, falls count anywhere, and Patterson pinned Brisco to become the new WWF hardcore champion. In one of pro wrestling's most ridiculous moments, Patterson and Brisco agreed to settle the score in a hardcore evening-gown match in which each man wore a dress.

9. **CHYNA**

In 1999, Chyna became the first woman to win the Intercontinental title. A few months later, Chyna was part of another first when she and Chris Jericho were both recognized as Intercontinental champions at the same time.

10. **MASTER SANDY**

Another female bodybuilder to win a title against males was Master Sandy. In August 1998, she challenged former Mr. USA Tony Atlas for the Eastern Wrestling Alliance title. It appeared to be a mismatch as Master Sandy was outweighed by nearly 100 pounds. During the match, Atlas was attacked by five of her bodybuilder friends. Once Atlas was softened up, Master Sandy pinned him to become the champion.

Short-Lived Champions

On April 27, 1981, Tommy "Wildfire" Rich defeated Harley Race to win the National Wrestling Alliance world title. Four days later, Race regained the belt. Since that time, Rich has been constantly reminded of his short title reign. The following wrestlers had even briefer stints as champions.

1. STING

On April 26, 1999, Sting won the WCW world title for the fifth time. Later that night, Diamond Dallas Page regained the belt in a four-way match with Sting, Kevin Nash, and Goldberg.

2. YOKOZUNA

Yokozuna defeated Bret Hart on April 4, 1993, to win the WWF world title. Immediately following his victory, Yokozuna's manager, Mr. Fuji, agreed to give Hulk Hogan a title shot that night. Hogan made the most of the opportunity by defeating Yokozuna to win the WWF title for a record fifth time.

3. KEVIN NASH

On January 25, 2000, acting WCW commissioner Kevin Nash stripped Sid Vicious of the world title and awarded it to himself. Later that night Vicious reclaimed the title.

4. KANE

Kane won the WWF world title on June 28, 1998, by prevailing in The King of the Ring tournament. The next day he lost the title to Stone Cold Steve Austin.

5. BRET HART

A final-four match was staged on February 16, 1997, in Knoxville, Tennessee, to determine the new World Wrestling Federation champion. The match became necessary when champion Shawn Michaels forfeited the belt. Bret Hart emerged victorious but lost the belt the next day to Sycho Sid.

6. MANKIND

Mankind won the WWF world title for the third time on August 22, 1999, in a match refereed by Minnesota governor Jesse Ventura. The next night Mankind lost the belt to Triple H.

7. RANDY SAVAGE

Randy Savage holds the dubious distinction of having two of the shortest title reigns in the history of World Championship Wrestling. The Macho Man defeated Sting on April 19, 1998, only to lose the belt to Hollywood Hogan the next day. On July 11, 1999, Savage defeated Kevin Nash to win the WCW heavyweight championship for the fourth time. Once again he lost the title to Hogan a day later.

8. THE ROCK

The Rock defeated Mankind on January 24, 1999, to win the WWF world title. Two nights later, Mankind regained his belt.

9. BOB BACKLUND

Bob Backlund's first two WWF title reigns lasted one year and four years. His third was considerably shorter. Backlund won the title for the third time from Bret Hart on November 23, 1994. Three days later, he lost it to Diesel in a match that lasted only six seconds.

10. CHRIS JERICHO

Chris Jericho's reign as World Wrestling Federation champion was so short that it was not officially recognized. In 2000, he cleanly defeated Triple H to become the WWF world champion. After the match, Triple H bullied the referee, causing him to reverse the decision.

Not Everyone Can Be a World Champion

For most professional wrestlers, winning a world title is just a dream. None of the following wrestlers won an individual world title, but each left his mark on pro wrestling.

1. STEVE LOMBARDI

In pro wrestling, Steve Lombardi is to losing what Hulk Hogan is to winning. The ultimate jobber in the World Wrestling Federation, Lombardi lost to champions and chumps. When he unveiled his Brooklyn Brawler character in the 1980s, there was hope that his luck might change. The Brawler began auspiciously by knocking Gorilla Monsoon senseless during a WWF broadcast, but soon the man in the torn jeans and New York sweatshirt was back to his losing ways. In July 2000, The Brooklyn Brawler came out of retirement to wrestle former WWF champion Triple H. Chris Jericho attacked Triple H during the match, enabling The Brooklyn Brawler to pull off one of the biggest upsets in pro-wrestling history.

2. **BARRY HOROWITZ**

Barry Horowitz rivaled Steve Lombardi as the WWF's premier jobber. A champion in lesser federations, Horowitz usually gave a good account of himself before his inevitable defeat. On those few occasions when he got the upper hand in a match, Horowitz congratulated himself by patting himself on the back. A few moments later, his back was usually pinned to the mat.

3. **SNAKE BROWN**

Some people are bad losers. Others are good losers. Snake Brown was a great loser. During the 1980s, Brown's screams of agony could be heard in arenas throughout the country. When an opponent clamped a hold on him, you could hear Brown yell, "The guy's killing me."

4. **MIKE JACKSON**

Mike Jackson was another grappler in the National Wrestling Alliance during the 1980s whose job it was to improve the won-loss records of his opponents. A skilled wrestler, Jackson was usually overpowered by larger foes. Unlike Snake Brown, Jackson went about his work in a quiet, professional manner.

5. **LES THATCHER**

Les Thatcher personified the journeyman wrestler. He toured throughout the Midwest and Southeast during the 1960s and 1970s. A solid performer, he once wrestled to a 50-minute draw with the highly regarded Danny Hodge. Today, Thatcher runs a wrestling school, Main Event, in Cincinnati.

A developer of future wrestling stars, Thatcher has been featured in behind-the-scenes wrestling segments on MTV's *Real Life* and ABC's *20/20*.

6. MAN MOUNTAIN CANNON

Wrestling fans of the 1960s will remember a 400-pound wrestler named George "Man Mountain" Cannon. Cannon had his greatest success as a manager of such tag teams as The Internationals, The Fabulous Kangaroos, and The Aryans. Cannon was nicknamed "Crybaby" because he didn't handle defeat very well.

7. JACKIE FARGO

Jackie Fargo was a favorite in the South and Midwest during the 1960s and 1970s. "The Fabulous One" was known for his stylish wrestling moves and his infectious personality.

8. THE MAGNIFICENT MURACO

Although he never won a world title, Don Muraco was a top contender in the WWF during the 1980s. The Magnificent Muraco carried on feuds with a number of WWF stars, including Pedro Morales, Jimmy Snuka, and Bob Backlund. Muraco was unsuccessful in his quest for the WWF world title. However, he was a two-time Intercontinental champion.

9. THE MIGHTY IGOR

The Mighty Igor was one of the strongest men in wrestling during the 1960s. However, the childlike strongman was lost without the guidance of his manager, Ivan Kalmikoff. During a match against his hated rival, The Sheik, Igor appeared to be on his way to victory. Without warning, Igor wandered off to find his manager, who had been injured earlier by the Sheik. As the Sheik lay helpless on the mat, Mighty Igor was counted out by the referee when he didn't return.

10. **BULLDOG BROWER**

One of the Mighty Igor's rivals for the title of the strongest man in wrestling was Bulldog Brower. He was known as the man with the Brower Power. Brower's detractors called him "The All-American Blowhard" because of his shameless self-promotion.

Hardcore Icons

Hardcore wrestling has become extremely popular in recent years. The no-disqualification, falls-count-anywhere matches have created legions of hardcore fans. Both the WWF and WCW now have hardcore champions, and every match in the ECW could be considered hardcore.

1. MICK FOLEY

Mick Foley has earned his reputation as the greatest hardcore wrestler of all time. In 1995, Foley was victorious in The King of the Death Match Tournament in Japan. In the finals, he defeated Terry Funk, his principal rival as the hardcore icon. Foley's complete disregard for his own health made him especially dangerous in hardcore matches. During his career, Foley had part of his right ear torn off, suffered a broken jaw, a broken cheekbone, a fractured nose, six cracked ribs, six concussions, and has had over 300 stitches. And you should have seen the other guys.

2. TERRY FUNK

If they gave a lifetime-achievement award for hardcore wrestling, Terry Funk would be the undisputed winner. He was wrestling hardcore matches before they had a name for them. He once left his mark on Kevin Nash with his Double Cross branding iron. As Chainsaw Charlie, he wrestled Cactus Jack in a fall-counts-anywhere match, which ended up with both wrestlers in a dumpster. In 2000, at the age of fifty-five, Funk defeated Shane "The Franchise" Douglas to win the WCW hardcore title. He wrestled that match in a gorilla outfit to conceal his identity.

3. SABU

Sabu has been called "The King of the Hardcore Matches." For a time in Extreme Championship Wrestling, the wildman was brought to the ring in a straightjacket. He will do anything to hurt an opponent, even if it means seriously injuring himself. Sabu's arms and chest are covered with scars, reminders of past barbed-wire matches. He broke his jaw and lost several teeth when he did a triple moonsault head-first into a table.

4. HARDCORE HOLLY

Bob Holly was a talented scientific wrestler before he transformed himself in the late 1990s into a hardcore specialist. Holly won the WWF hardcore title in 1999.

5. CRASH HOLLY

Bob Holly's little cousin, Crash Holly, has established himself as a hardcore star. He claims to be over 400 pounds, although, in reality, he weighs about half that much. He usually carried a scale to the ring to try to prove he was really that heavy. In February 2000, Crash won the WWF hardcore title. Since falls count anywhere, anytime, Holly was constantly on the run from other wrestlers eager to take his title.

6. THE SANDMAN

The Sandman is known as The Original Hardcore Icon. The ECW legend has used his rattan cane to put many wrestlers to sleep.

7. KEVIN SULLIVAN

Kevin Sullivan was one of the toughest hardcore competitors in wrestling history. In one memorable match against The Canadian Crippler Chris Benoit, the two men battled throughout the arena—in the stands, at concession booths, even in the bathroom.

8. THE BIG BOSS MAN

The Big Boss Man is a four-time WWF hardcore champion. The 320-pound former prison guard defeated Mankind to win the belt the first time. Whenever possible, he attacks opponents with his nightstick.

9. AL SNOW

Al Snow has the perfect mentality for a hardcore wrestler. His unpredictability makes him difficult to wrestle. The three-time WWF hardcore champion is at his best outside the ring, where he can bash an opponent with a chair, table, or garbage can.

10. TIGER JEET SINGH

No one is more dangerous in a hardcore match than Tiger
Jeet Singh. Although he lost in the semifinals of The King of
the Death Match Tournament in 1995, Singh proved his ability against much younger competitors. His hardcore style
made him a fan favorite in Japan.

Lights Out

These wrestlers could really pack a punch.

1. PRIMO CARNERA

Primo Carnera knocked out Jack Sharkey to win the heavy-weight boxing championship of the world in 1933. It was one of 68 knockouts in Carnera's boxing career. After he retired from boxing, Carnera became a professional wrestler. He won an astounding 321 matches in a row before losing to Antonino Rocca in 1949.

2. WILD BULL CURRY

In 1940, Bull Curry fought an exhibition against former heavyweight champion Jack Dempsey. Curry always claimed he knocked out Dempsey. However, the record book shows Bull was stopped in the second round. As a wrestler, Curry's offensive arsenal consisted of a powerful right hand. His punches were certainly the most deliberate in wrestling history. Nearing the end of his career in the 1970s, Curry claimed he could still knock out Muhammad Ali and Joe Frazier.

3. STAN STASIAK

Stan "The Man" Stasiak was the master of the heart punch. When he delivered his blow with his taped fist, opponents would instantly collapse. Stasiak defeated Pedro Morales to win the WWF world title in 1973.

4. MARC MERO

Marc Mero had an amateur boxing background. As either Johnny B. Badd or Marvelous Marc Mero, he put away many opponents with his powerful punch. Some thought that his wife, Rena, was the real knockout in the family.

5. THUNDERBOLT PATTERSON

Thunderbolt Patterson called himself "The Man's Threat and the Woman's Pet." The African-American star of the 1970s won many matches with a deadly heart punch.

6. SPECIAL DELIVERY JONES

Special Delivery Jones was a WWF stalwart in the 1980s. A tough competitor, Jones used head butts and a knockout punch to win matches.

7. THE CRUSHER

The Crusher was a brawler who often got himself into toe-to-toe slugfests with his opponents. He would begin with a windmill motion to deliver his bolo punch, which he used to knock out opponents.

8. **BRUISER BENNETT**

Bruiser Bennett was a popular wrestler in Texas in the late 1990s. His heart punch finisher is known as Cardiac Arrest.

9. **JIMMY WOODSTOCK**

Jimmy Woodstock is a 300-pound wrestler who debuted in the late 1990s. Known as The Love Child, Woodstock named his version of the heart punch The Punch of Love.

10. **MAJOR DE BEERS**

Major De Beers has held numerous brass-knuckles titles around the country. The moustached South African heel has one of the best heart punches in the business.

Wildmen

Take a walk on the wild side of professional wrestling.

1. WILD BULL CURRY

Wild Bull Curry caused riots wherever he wrestled. Barred from many arenas, he was involved in some of the dirtiest matches of all time. Most ended outside the ring, with Curry picking up a chair or whatever he could lay his hands on. Curry often used brass knuckles to make his punches even more damaging. Totally out of control, The Bull salivated and grunted during his rampages. During a 1961 match, Curry chased Bulldog Brower through the streets of Halifax. Brower jumped into an automobile just as Curry broke the windshield with a two-by-four.

2. PAMPERO FIRPO

Pampero Firpo was known as The Wild Bull of the Pampas. The Argentine had bushy black hair, a full beard, and a voice which resembled Cookie Monster's. His encounters with The Sheik are among the wildest matches on record.

3. THE MISSING LINK

One of the most bizarre wrestlers of the 1980s, The Missing Link was billed as half-man, half-animal. The Wildman wore green paint on his face. He had a small tuft of hair in front and a larger clump of black hair on the back of his head. It was said that he lived in the wild like an animal, foraging for fruit and eating live alligators. He disabled his opponents with butts from his rock-hard head.

4. THE SHEIK

No list of wrestling wildmen would be complete without The Sheik. The Madman from Syria savaged his opponents with pencils and other foreign objects he pulled from his trunks. He injured many wrestlers by throwing fire into their faces. The only wrestling hold he seemed to know was his Camel-Clutch Finisher.

5. ABDULLAH THE BUTCHER

The Sudanese Wildman, Abdullah the Butcher, may have been pro wrestling's most feared opponent. For more than forty years, The Butcher has treated opponents like they were pieces of meat. Using a variety of foreign objects to tear open opponents' foreheads, he finished them off by dropping a vicious elbow on their throats.

6. KAMALA

Kamala the Ugandan Headhunter had many similarities to Abdullah the Butcher. Both men weighed over 350 pounds. Each one was completely uncontrollable in the ring. Kamala and Abdullah came from countries in Africa. Most disturbing were their claims of being cannibals.

7. GEORGE "THE ANIMAL" STEELE

George Steele never claimed to be a cannibal, but he was fond of eating turnbuckle protectors. The Animal bit them until the posts were exposed so he could ram his opponents' heads into the metal. Always appearing to be in another world, Steele would stick his tongue out of the side of his mouth and gaze into space with a crazed look.

8. THE BARBARIAN

The 300-pound Barbarian waged a campaign of destruction throughout the past two decades. He was particularly effective in tag-team action. The Barbarian frequently teamed with the equally intimidating Meng. He also teamed with The Warlord to form The Powers of Pain.

9. JEFF ANDERSON

Known as The Wildman, Jeff Anderson has displayed his brand of mayhem mainly on the Southern independent circuit. He and Tony Anthony were a tag team known as Wild and Dirty.

10. SKINNER

Skinner was one of the more unpleasant wrestlers in the WWF during the early 1990s. The Man from the Everglades stalked his opponents like a hunter closing in on his prey. The bearded backwoodsman threatened to skin his opponents alive and tack their hides to the wall of his trophy room.

Soul Takers and Undertakers

Some wrestlers have summoned their powers from the occult. Take a look at wrestling's dark side.

1. THE UNDERTAKER

The Undertaker made his first appearance in the WWF in 1990 and has been raising hell ever since. Accompanied by his manager, Paul Bearer, The Undertaker zipped up his defeated foes in body bags. According to the story line, he was born in Death Valley and raised in a funeral parlor. A master of the casket match (in which the loser is placed in a casket), the Undertaker is a three-time WWF champ. Wrestlers don't get up from his tombstone pile driver. The Undertaker, on the other hand, is nearly indestructible. When it appears that he is unconscious, he will unexpectedly sit up. The leader of The Ministry of Darkness once "crucified" The Big Boss Man. In 1996, he popped through the bottom of the mat and dragged Diesel to "hell." He warned his opponents, "You will rest in peace."

2. KEVIN SULLIVAN

If you believe Kevin Sullivan, he's on a first-name basis with Satan. He came to the ring dressed in a black cloak and hood. Sullivan was accompanied by his cult of satanic worshippers, including the attractive but deadly Fallen Angel. For Kevin Sullivan, it was more important to hurt an opponent than to win, making a match with him a hellish experience.

3. PAPA SHANGO

Papa Shango was the master of voodoo. He took his name from the voodoo god of power. Wrestling's soul taker wore a necklace of bones and waved a skull that had smoke emanating from its eye sockets. He put spells on wrestlers so that their souls would suffer as much as their bodies from the punishment he inflicted on them. Papa Shango had evil magical powers and once set Johnny Paradise's hands on fire.

4. DEMON HELLSTROM

Demon Hellstrom was the Sunshine Wrestling Federation champion in the late 1990s. His disposition is anything but sunny. The demon claims to be from the "bowels of hell."

5. MIDEON

Mideon became a member of the Undertaker's Ministry of Darkness after being kidnapped by The Acolytes. His soul was sacrificed in a bizarre ceremony. Going over to the dark side, he carried an eye with him. His finishing move was called The Eye Opener.

6. RAVEN

Raven won the ECW world title in 1996. The leader of The Flock spoke in poetic cadences and maintained a gothic persona inspired by Edgar Allan Poe. He ended each of his rambling monologues with the word "nevermore." During a stint in the WCW, he was part of The Dead Pool with Vampiro and The Insane Clown Posse. A hardcore specialist, he finished off his opponents with an evenflow DDT.

7. THE SINISTER MINISTER

An addition to the ECW in the year 2000, The Sinister Minister is the devil incarnate. Dressed in a red jacket, he is accompanied by his crimson-haired toadie, Mikey Whipwreck. With his devilish laugh, he is usually up to some kind of mischief.

8. LORD CULT

Lord Cult held regional belts in New England during the 1990s. The lord of darkness used black magic to help him win matches.

9. THE MUMMY

Talk about a wrestler under wraps. The Mummy, who wrestled in Texas during the 1960s, was wrapped in bandages from head to toe.

10. APOCALYPSE

The Christian Wrestling Federation based in Texas uses wrestling as a vehicle to proselytize. Matches are parables of good and evil. Wrestlers named The Saint and The Martyr battle for the salvation of mankind. The most popular star of the federation is a high-flying wrestler named Angel. A burly wrestler called Apocalypse is the personification of evil. After the matches have concluded, the wrestlers preach the gospel to the crowd.

Bloodthirsty Wrestlers

The following wrestlers have an unquenchable thirst for blood.

1. GANGREL

Formerly known as The Vampire Warrior, Gangrel drinks from a chalice and spits a blood-like substance before his matches. A member of The Brood, he gave his opponents bloodbaths as buckets of blood were poured on them from the rafters. Although the gothic wrestler has fangs, he rarely bites opponents.

2. VAMPIRO

Vampiro became a major force in WCW in the year 2000. During a match between Sting and Jeff Jarrett, Vampiro reached up through the mat and pulled down The Stinger. When Sting emerged, he was covered with blood. Vampiro became Vampyro when he burned Sting in a human-torch match at The Great American Bash. His finishing moves are The Nail in the Coffin and Vampire Spike.

3. VAMPIRO AMERICANO

Justin Bradshaw was known as Vampiro Americano briefly in the 1980s. He gained greater fame in the 1990s as one-half of the WWF tag team champions, The Acolytes.

4. FRED BLASSIE

Pro wrestling's true vampire was Fred Blassie. Blassie used to file his teeth before a match to make them razor sharp. He usually sank his fangs into the victim's forehead to start the blood flowing. His bloodthirsty style made him a legend in Japan.

5. ABDULLAH THE BUTCHER

For Abdullah the Butcher, the wrestling ring is his abattoir. One opponent said that when Abdullah sees blood, he is like a shark going into a feeding frenzy. As a member of The Seventh Tribe of Sudan, he reportedly took part in a ritual in which he killed a cow with his own hands and drank some of its blood.

6. THE HEADHUNTERS

Imagine two Abdullah the Butchers and you have the tag team The Headhunters. The two men not only physically resemble The Butcher, but they share his incredible lust for blood.

7. YOSHI KWAN

Yoshi Kwan practiced his peculiar form of bloodletting mostly in the South during the 1990s. Two of his favorite methods of cutting opponents were slicing them with a samurai sword and gouging their faces with his sharp fingernails.

8. ABBUDAH SINGH

Abbudah Singh is a 300-pound madman who has been involved in some of the bloodiest matches in pro-wrestling history. His feud with Abdullah the Butcher can be best described as a gorefest.

9. COUNT DRACULA

The wrestler Count Dracula named himself after the original vampire. Rather than hypnotizing his victims, he carried a bottle of chloroform to knock them out.

10. MAXX CRIMSON

Maxx Crimson's name tells you all you need to know about his attitude toward bloodletting. "The Outlaw" proudly admits that his rulebreaking has gotten him banned in over thirty states.

Foreign Objects

The use of foreign objects is one of the most dangerous aspects of professional wrestling. These wrestlers frequently used foreign objects to injure their opponents.

1. ABDULLAH THE BUTCHER

The undisputed "Master of the Foreign Object," Abdullah the Butcher has used forks, knives, razor blades, spikes, and anything else he could lay his hands on to carve his mark into the foreheads of his unfortunate opponents. The Butcher once pulled a screwdriver from his tights in a match against Blackjack Mulligan, but his greatest atrocity came against Cowboy Scott Casey. Abdullah used a fork to turn Casey into a bloody mess in one of the most barbaric moments in the history of professional wrestling.

2. NEW JACK

New Jack teamed with Mustafa Saed to form a tag team known as The Gangstas. They won ECW tag-team titles in

1996 and 1997. New Jack brings a garbage can full of foreign objects to the ring. He has pulled everything out of the can from a staple gun to a sickle.

3. THE SHEIK

Almost no match went by without The Sheik pulling a foreign object from his trunks. His favorites were a sharp pencil that he used to jab an opponent's forehead and throat and a flashboard which allowed him to throw fire into his foe's face.

4. HACKSAW JIM DUGGAN

Hacksaw Jim Duggan is that rare wrestler who remained a fan favorite despite the flagrant use of a foreign object. Duggan carries a two-by-four to the ring with him and is not shy about using it.

5. STING

Sting brings a different piece of wood to the ring. Often attacked by members of The New World Order, Sting carries a baseball bat that he calls "The Equalizer."

6. AXL ROTTEN

Axl Rotten is "The King of the Foreign Object Matches." The bloody Brit's weapon of choice is a barbed-wire-covered baseball bat.

7. THE ONE MAN GANG

The One Man Gang is a 450-pound tough from the mean streets of Chicago. He lugs a steel chain that he uses to beat and choke his opponents.

8. THE MOUNTIE

The Mountie vowed to always get his man. When he couldn't subdue his opponents with wrestling moves, he resorted to a shock stick. The cattle prod was so effective that he defeated Bret Hart for the Intercontinental title in 1992.

9. LEX LUGER

Lex Luger's foreign object was beautifully concealed. He had a steel plate inserted into his right forearm following a motor-cycle accident. The Total Package used the flying-forearm smash to put away many of his opponents.

10. ROWDY RODDY PIPER

Rowdy Roddy Piper was known to employ a foreign object such as brass knuckles or a roll of quarters to drop opponents. This is how he flattened the great Andre the Giant during a tag-team match in the 1980s. The bloodied Giant was so badly hurt that he had to be carried out of the ring.

Props

Many wrestlers have used props as part of their routine.

1. AL SNOW

It shouldn't surprise anyone that Al Snow hears voices. Snow is one of wrestling's most eccentric characters. He had "Help Me" written on his forehead. Snow claimed that he received instructions from a female mannequin head that he carried with him. "Head" became his manager and constant companion.

2. MANKIND

Mankind's finishing move was a mandible claw that he applied to the inside of his opponent's mouth. To add insult to injury, he placed a dirty white sock on his hand before applying the hold. He named the sock "Mr. Socko."

3. CHAVO GUERRERO, JR.

Chavo Guerrero Jr. went crazy after weeks of physical and verbal abuse from his uncle, Eddy. He began riding a broomstick horse that he named Pepe. The broomstick steed met a bad end when Norman Smiley put Pepe in a wood chipper.

4. JIM CORNETTE

Jim Cornette was one of the most successful wrestling managers of the 1980s. His trademark was his tennis racket which he often used to whack rival wrestlers.

5. MARK SCHRADER

Mark "The Shark" Schrader was a pool hustler-turned wrestler who won many regional titles in the 1990s. He used his pool cue to break his opponents and chalked up many victories.

6. BOBBY DUNCUM, JR.

Like his father, Big Bad Bobby Duncum, Bobby Duncum, Jr. was a rugged competitor. Duncum frequently carried a bull rope and cowbell to the ring and used them on his opponents whenever possible.

7. THE HONKY TONK MAN

The Honky Tonk Man brought a guitar to the ring with him because he believed he was the second coming of Elvis. While he proved no threat to the King of Rock 'n' Roll, he found a better use for the instrument. In a move perfected by the cartoon character El Kabong, the Honky Tonk Man smashed his guitar over other wrestlers' heads. The move has been revived in recent years by another frustrated singer, Jeff Jarrett.

8. **ECW TABLE**

In Extreme Championship Wrestling, they use tables for everything but eating. Wrestlers set up tables in the corners, the middle, and outside the ring for the sole purpose of slamming their opponents through them.

9. **BRIAN DANZIG**

Brian Danzig has spent much of his career wrestling in the Southeast and Atlantic coast states. Although he's small for a professional wrestler, no one messes with him because he carries a chain wrapped in barbed wire.

10. **JIMMY HART**

If a poll was taken among wrestling fans for the all-time most irritating prop, the megaphone of manager Jimmy Hart would probably win. "The Mouth of the South" used the megaphone to distract referees, irritate opponents, and occasionally attack them.

Dirty Wrestlers

Fred Blassie once said that he couldn't understand why a wrestler went to the trouble of using a hold when it was much easier to disable a man by kicking him in the groin. In professional wrestling, a flagrant rulebreaker like Fred Blassie is known as a dirty wrestler. These ten guys are downright dirty.

1. DIRTY DICK SLATER

Dirty Dick Slater did whatever it took to win. If it meant biting, kicking, or choking an opponent, so be it. "I see no reason not to be mean and sadistic," he said. Slater teamed with Bunkhouse Buck to win the WCW tag-team title in 1995. In 1983, Slater was the United States wrestling champion.

2. DIRTY DICK RHINES

Slater was not the first "Dirty Dick" in professional wrestling. That distinction belonged to Dirty Dick Rhines, a star of the 1940s.

3. **DIRTY DICK MURDOCH**

Dirty Dick Murdoch was a star in both the WWF and NWA during the 1980s. Also known as "Captain Redneck," he teamed with Adrian Adonis to win the World Wrestling Federation tag-team belt in 1983.

4. **RIC FLAIR**

Ric Flair is often called "The Dirtiest Player in the Game." Many times Flair used brass knuckles to knock out an opponent. If Flair isn't the dirtiest player in the game, the seventeen-time world champion is certainly the most successful.

5. **TONY ANTHONY**

Tony Anthony was known as "The Dirty White Boy." He was married to Kimberly, "The Dirty White Girl." Anthony was part of a tag team known as Wild and Dirty. He had a brief stint in the World Wrestling Federation as T.L. Hopper, whose primary skill outside of wrestling was fixing toilets.

6. **THE FILTHY ANIMALS**

The Filthy Animals are an outlaw group in World Championship Wrestling. They are capable of anything from committing a mugging to stealing a wrestler's wallet. Some of the wrestlers who have been members of The Filthy Animals include Rey Misterio Jr., Konnan, Eddy Guerrero, Kidman, and The Disco Inferno.

7. **DIRTY DUTCH MANTEL**

Dirty Dutch Mantel has been a top performer in southern promotions for more than 25 years. In 1997, the veteran won the United States Wrestling Association heavyweight title.

8. DUKE "THE DUMPSTER" DROESE

Duke "The Dumpster" Droese is wrestling's trashman. The 300-pounder is always talking trash—or at least talking about trash. Droese's finishing move is called The Trash Compactor.

9. THE GODWINNS

The Godwinns, Henry and Phineas, were a tag team managed by Hillbilly Jim. The Godwinns were the WWF tag-team champions in 1996 and 1997. The wrestling hillbillies brought a bucket of slop to the ring with them.

10. RICK CONNERS

Rick Conners claims he knows every dirty trick in the book. For more than thirty years he was a rulebreaker on the southern circuit. Conners used brass knuckles whenever he could get away with it.

Wrestling Fanatics

Professional wrestling fans are among the most rabid in sports. Occasionally, a fan crosses the line. When that happens, someone gets hurt.

1. WILD BULL CURRY

Wild Bull Curry was a riot waiting to happen. In 1955, more than 140 fans in Atlanta were taken to hospitals after a riot broke out during a match between Curry and Ray McIntyre. A year later in Charlotte, North Carolina, a fan was so incensed by Curry's treatment of George Becker that he made the mistake of jumping into the ring to come to Becker's aid. Curry wheeled around and broke the man's jaw with one punch. In 1958, Curry was pounding Pepper Gomez in Galveston when a fan hit Bull over the head with an iron pipe. Curry chased the man into the balcony and beat him senseless. Ten years later in Worcester, Massachusetts, Curry was wrestling Emil Dupre when a fan jumped on his back. Curry punched the fan so hard that he was unconscious for two days.

2. DICK THE BRUISER

On November 18, 1957, Antonino Rocca and Edouard Carpentier wrestled against Dick the Bruiser and Dr. Jerry Graham in the main event at New York's Madison Square Garden. Dick the Bruiser's tactics so angered the fans that several of them jumped into the ring to attack him. The Bruiser tossed them out of the ring one-by-one and a riot ensued. Many spectators were injured during the melee. The New York Athletic Commission ruled that if it happened again, professional wrestling would be banned from Madison Square Garden.

3. FRED BLASSIE

One of wrestling's most hated heels, Fred Blassie was a target for fans. In one match, Blassie felt a pain in his leg. When he looked down he was horrified to see a knife sticking in his leg. On another occasion, a fan threw acid on his leg. When Blassie pulled down his sock in the dressing room, his skin came off.

4. BLACKJACK MULLIGAN

Blackjack Mulligan was a victim of a vicious knife attack by a fan in Boston. The man cut Mulligan's leg so severely that more than 100 stitches were required to close the wound.

5. PAUL ORNDORFF

Paul Orndorff had an evening he'd rather forget in Pennsylvania in 1984. Outside the ring, a fan hit Mr. Wonderful from behind. When Orndorff turned around to take a swing at him, he missed the assailant and struck an elderly man in the face, knocking out his dentures.

6. DANNY HODGE

Danny Hodge was stabbed in the back by a fan during a match in Oklahoma City. What made the attack more painful was that the assailant was Hodge's father.

7. CAPTAIN LOU ALBANO

Manager Lou Albano recalled the time that he was slashed on the arm by a fan in Washington, D.C. He was being chased by Bruno Sammartino through the crowd when the attack occurred.

8. ART NEILSON

Art Neilson, one-half of the champion Neilson Brothers tag team, was the victim of a knife attack in Chattanooga, Tennessee. Stabbed in the side by a fan, he underwent emergency surgery.

9. ROWDY RODDY PIPER

Rowdy Roddy Piper was once stabbed in the parking lot by a fan. The resourceful Piper said that he'd sustained the injury while trying to save children from a knife-wielding maniac.

10. ARTURO TOSCANINI

Arturo Toscanini was a famed classical music conductor and a rabid wrestling fan. In his eighties, the conductor of the NBC Symphony Orchestra, was watching wrestling on television and yelled "Kill him!" when one of the heels was taking a beating.

Grudge Matches

A grudge match occurs when two wrestlers get involved in a feud. Some grudges never get settled and can last for years. Here are some of pro wrestling's greatest grudge matches.

1. HULK HOGAN VS. RODDY PIPER

Hulk Hogan was The King of Wrestling during the 1980s. The WWF champion was the most popular wrestler of all time. His nemesis was Roddy Piper, the consummate heel. Hogan and Mr. T were matched against Piper and Paul Orndorff in the main event of the first Wrestlemania in 1985. A decade later, the two old rivals clashed again, this time in World Championship Wrestling. Hogan was the champion, but he had turned heel and Piper was the fan favorite. Piper won the first match with his sleeper hold and again had Hogan in the sleeper during the rematch when Randy Savage interfered to cost Piper the match.

2. THE SHEIK VS. DICK THE BRUISER

The Sheik battled Dick the Bruiser in arenas throughout the country during the 1960s and 1970s. What made their rivalry so unusual for the time was that both wrestlers were heels. Up until that time, heels were almost always matched against babyfaces. The bouts between the man known as the "Maniac of the Mat" and "The World's Most Dangerous Wrestler" were action-packed classics.

3. THE ROCK VS. TRIPLE H

The World Wrestling Federation reached a new peak in popularity during the last few years. One of the reasons for the renewed popularity was the rivalry between The Rock and Hunter Hearst Helmsley. The feud intensified when Triple H married Stephanie McMahon and won the WWF title. Helmsley used his influence to frustrate The Rock's attempt to regain the title. Finally in 2000, The Rock was able to win the belt from Triple H, but the rivalry should continue for years to come.

4. ANDRE THE GIANT VS. BIG JOHN STUDD

At seven feet, four inches tall and weighing over 500 pounds, Andre the Giant was so huge that few men were a match for him. That didn't stop Big John Studd from considering himself to be the true giant of professional wrestling. The two giants met in a series of matches, including a body-slam match won by Andre. Studd was never able to beat Andre, but he was the wrestler who came the closest until Hulk Hogan finally pinned Andre at Wrestlemania III.

5. ABDULLAH THE BUTCHER VS. CARLOS COLON

The longest-running feud in professional wrestling was also the bloodiest. Abdullah the Butcher and Carlos Colon have been involved in some of the wildest matches ever seen. No ring can hold them. Their wild brawls spill out into the crowd. The Butcher has used everything from bells to micro-phones to inflict punishment on Colon. "I've suffered more cuts and broken bones in matches against Abdullah than against anyone else," Colon lamented.

6. STEVE AUSTIN VS. VINCE MCMAHON

The most unlikely rivalry in wrestling was that between Stone Cold Steve Austin and WWF chairman Vince McMahon. Austin was the WWF's most popular wrestler when McMahon began to antagonize The Texas Rattlesnake. Eventually, McMahon agreed to wrestle Austin. While the matches were decidedly in Austin's favor, the ingenious story line helped propel the WWF into a dominant position in professional wrestling.

7. FRED BLASSIE VS. JOHN TOLOS

A memorable feud took place on the West Coast in the 1960s between Fred Blassie and John Tolos. Blassie, one of the most hated men in all of professional wrestling, had changed his ways and become a fan favorite. Tolos, known as "The Golden Greek," was skeptical of the transformation. The two men engaged in a series of bloody battles. One night Tolos brought a large red box into the ring. He promised that the contents of the box would put an end to Blassie's career. When Blassie opened the box, he was horrified to discover a huge python. Blassie reverted to his old style and sank his teeth into Tolos's forehead. He gave Tolos a terrible beating before pinning him.

8. THE UNDERTAKER VS. KANE

The Biblical story of Cain and Abel was resurrected in the wres-tling ring as Kane arrived in the World Wrestling Federation to seek vengeance on his brother, The Undertaker. According to the story, as a child The Undertaker started a fire that seriously burned Kane. Kane wore a red and black mask to cover his disfigured face. Paul Bearer, The Undertaker's manager, switched allegiance to Kane. The two big men had almost identical wrestling styles, so it was almost like watching mirror images fight.

9. ROB VAN DAM VS. JERRY LYNN

Extreme Championship Wrestling is known for its grudge matches, but none lasted longer than that of Rob Van Dam and Jerry Lynn. Lynn, an up-and-coming star, was one of the few wrestlers who could match Van Dam move-for-move. It seemed as though the two wrestled every week for Van Dam's television title. Finally, at the Hardcore Heaven 2000 pay-per-view, Lynn won the belt.

10. SGT. SLAUGHTER VS. THE IRON SHEIK

The rivalry between Sgt. Slaughter and The Iron Sheik took many turns over the years. Slaughter was an ex-drill instructor and American patriot. The Iron Sheik was from Iran and was an ardent follower of the Ayatollah. These men waged war during the 1980s. In 1990, the feud took an unexpected turn when Slaughter formed an alliance with The Sheik. With The Sheik's assistance, Sgt. Slaughter won the WWF world title in 1991. After Slaughter lost the title to Hulk Hogan, he renewed his feud with The Iron Sheik.

Memorable Matches

Every wrestling fan has his own favorite match. My personal favorite was a two-out-of-three match between The Sheik and Fred Blassie, which took place at Cincinnati Gardens in the mid-1960s. It was the only time I could ever remember The Sheik being the crowd favorite. The two wild men traded falls, with the third fall ending in a double disqualification. Here are ten of pro wrestling's most memorable matches.

1. THE UNDERTAKER VS. MANKIND

The reputation of the 1998 Hell in the Cell II match between the Undertaker and Mankind will continue to grow. The two men fought on top of a fifteen-foot-high steel cage. Fans were horrified when the Undertaker threw Mankind off the top of the cage. He landed on the Spanish announcer's table (a running joke in the WWF—the Spanish announcer's table is always destroyed during the pay-per-view). It was assumed that Mankind was seriously injured and the match was over. He was being carried to the dressing room for medical assistance when he got off the stretcher and climbed back up the cage. The Undertaker choke-slammed Mankind, who fell through the top of the cage and landed on the mat below. Amazingly, the match continued. Mankind had survived two fifteen-foot falls but could not get up from a tombstone pile driver. Mick Foley suffered a dislocated jaw, broken ribs and ankle, and had a tooth driven through his nose by the impact of his falls. Ironically, the three-time WWF champion will best be remembered for a match he lost.

2.   BOB BACKLUND VS. JIMMY SNUKA

Mick Foley's wrestling hero was Superfly Jimmy Snuka. The match which has the biggest influence on him was a 1982 encounter between Snuka and WWF champion Bob Backlund. Snuka had given Backlund serious beatings in their previous encounters but was unable to win the belt. Finally, they agreed to a cage match to settle the score. It appeared Snuka was going to win the title when he climbed to the top of the cage for his famed splash. Backlund got out of the way just in time and retained his title, but it was Snuka who gained fans for his incredible leap.

3.   HULK HOGAN VS. ANDRE THE GIANT

The matchup between WWF champion Hulk Hogan and Andre the Giant at Wrestlemania III was the most anticipated in wrestling history. Andre the Giant had never been clearly defeated, but he had also never been WWF champion. More than 93,000 fans jammed the Pontiac Silverdome to witness wrestling history. Hogan became the first man to body-slam the 500-pound Giant and pinned him to become the undisputed king of wrestling.

4. CACTUS JACK VS. TERRY FUNK

Cactus Jack met Terry Funk in the finals of the 1995 King of
the Death Match tournament in Tokyo. The tournament can
best be described as a torture show. The two men had survived bloody battles to reach the finale. Bloodied and ban-
daged, they met in a ring surrounded by barbed wire and
booby-trapped with explosives. Cactus Jack won the match
with the help of outside interference from Tiger Jeet Singh.
The winner had fifty stitches in his face, ear, and arm to
show for his victory, but it earned him the reputation as the
greatest hardcore wrestler who ever lived.

5. RIC FLAIR

Ric Flair has had many triumphs in wrestling, but his finest
moment may have come at the 1992 Royal Rumble. The
winner of the thirty-man battle royal would become the new
WWF champion. Despite being one of the first wrestlers to
enter the ring, Flair outlasted the greatest stars in the WWF
to win the world heavyweight title.

6. HULK HOGAN VS. THE IRON SHEIK

The 1984 WWF championship match between The Iron Sheik
and Hulk Hogan will forever be remembered as the coronation of The Hulkster. The Iron Sheik had just defeated longtime champion Bob Backlund for the belt. When Backlund
was unable to appear in a return match because of an injury,
Hogan was selected as his replacement. When the Iron Sheik
pulled Hogan's head back in his dreaded cobra-clutch submission hold, you could hear a pin drop in the arena.
Amazingly, Hogan rose and pushed The Sheik back into the

ropes. A few moments later, Hogan pinned The Sheik to become WWF champion.

7. BUDDY ROGERS VS. PAT O'CONNOR

The 1961 two-out-of-three-falls NWA title match between champion Pat O'Connor and Nature Boy Buddy Rogers was a milestone in wrestling history. More than 38,000 fans packed Chicago's Comiskey Park. In the third and deciding fall, O'Connor missed a drop kick and injured his groin, allowing Rogers to pin him to become the new NWA champion.

8. HULK HOGAN AND MR. T VS. RODDY PIPER AND PAUL ORNDORFF

The main event of Wrestlemania I was significant for many reasons. It featured WWF champion Hulk Hogan and bodyguard-turned-actor Mr. T against Roddy Piper and Mr. Wonderful Paul Orndorff. Wrestlemania I was the first major wrestling pay-per-view and the success of this match was instrumental in launching these special events, which revolutionized the industry. It also introduced the celebrity connection, which has helped transform wrasslin' into sports entertainment. By the way, Hogan and Mr. T emerged victorious.

9. RODDY PIPER VS. GREG VALENTINE

The feud between Roddy Piper and Greg Valentine was one of the fiercest of the 1980s. The two men took turns winning the United States title. The seesaw affair culminated in a dog-collar match at the Greensboro Coliseum. The two men wore dog collars linked by a steel chain. Piper and Valentine used the chain to beat each other into bloody pulps. Piper finally ended the carnage by pinning Valentine.

10. NIKOLAI VOLKOFF VS. GORILLA MONSOON

Four-hundred-pound Gorilla Monsoon had been the enforcer in the WWF. Anyone who wanted a shot at Bruno Sammartino's world title had to go through him. In 1971, a huge Russian named Nikolai Volkoff challenged Monsoon. Volkoff decisively defeated Monsoon in a match that lasted only four minutes. Although he never won the WWF title, the match launched Volkoff's long career and relegated Monsoon to trial-horse status.

Old Wrestlers Never Die

Unlike most athletes, professional wrestlers often remain active well into their fifties.

1. LOU THESZ

Lou Thesz won his first world title in 1937 and was still a champion in the 1960s. He stayed in remarkable shape and wrestled into his seventies.

2. WILD BULL CURRY

One writer accused Bull Curry of being on the undercard of David and Goliath. Curry vowed to die with his wrestling boots on, and he almost did, remaining active well past his sixtieth birthday.

3. ABDULLAH THE BUTCHER

Abdullah the Butcher debuted in 1958 and four decades later was still busting heads. In a recent legends match against the One-Man Gang, he showed he hadn't lost his touch by repeatedly jabbing a fork into his opponent's forehead.

4. DICK THE BRUISER

Dick the Bruiser began wrestling in the 1950s, following a pro-football career with the Green Bay Packers. He was over sixty and still wrestling when he suffered a fatal injury while weightlifting.

5. THE GIANT BABA

The Giant Baba was a champion in both the United States and Japan. His career spanned nearly forty years, and he wrestled until his death in the late 1990s.

6. PAT PATTERSON

Pat Patterson was the first Intercontinental champion in 1979. In 2000, the fifty-eight-year-old Patterson won the WWF hardcore title.

7. TERRY FUNK

Ageless Terry Funk continues to show why he is a hardcore legend. In 2000, the fifty-five-year-old Texan won the WCW hardcore title. Three years earlier, Funk reigned as the ECW world champion.

8. DORY FUNK, JR.

Dory Funk, Jr. may be less visible than his brother Terry, but he also has had one of the sport's longest careers. Funk first won the NWA world title in 1963 and was still active in the late 1990s.

9. **RIC FLAIR**

Even other wrestlers joke about how old Ric Flair is. The story lines have Flair suffering heart attacks and other serious physical ailments. In 2000, he had his head shaven and was forced to retire after losing a match. We'll see how long the retirement lasts.

10. **GEORGE STEELE**

George "The Animal" Steele has unleashed his peculiar form of mayhem in wrestling rings for nearly forty years. A star in the WWF in the 1970s and 1980s, he still occasionally wrestles on the independent circuit and in legends matches.

They Died Too Soon

Professional wrestling has had more than its share of athletes who died before their time. That long list has included promising performers such as Bobby Duncum, Jr. and Rick McGraw.

1. THE VON ERICHS

The saga of the Von Erich family is almost too tragic to believe. Fritz von Erich was a world champion in the 1960s. He had five sons, all of whom had promising wrestling careers. In 1984, David von Erich died of an intestinal hemorrhage during a tour of Japan. Three years later, his brother Mike committed suicide. In 1991, twenty-one-year-old Chris von Erich also took his own life. Perhaps the most tragic story concerned Kerry von Erich. Kerry had won the NWA world title from Ric Flair in 1984. His future seemed to have no limits when he severely injured his ankle in a motorcycle accident. The injury eventually resulted in his right foot being amputated. Despite the handicap, Kerry von Erich was able to win the Intercontinental title in 1990. The constant pain and disappointment proved too much for Kerry, and he, too, committed suicide in 1993. Only Kevin remained of the five von Erich brothers.

2. OWEN HART

Many wrestlers have died in the ring, but none so tragically as Owen Hart. On May 23, 1999, he was scheduled to appear as The Blue Blazer in a match against The Godfather in Kansas City's Kemper Arena during the Over the Edge pay-per-view. He was supposed to make his appearance by rappelling from the rafters, but somehow, he got detached from the safety harness and fell more than fifty feet to his death.

3. BRUISER BRODY

Bruiser Brody was stabbed to death in Puerto Rico in July 1988. Reportedly, he was stabbed in the abdomen by Jose Gonzalez, a wrestler and promoter. Gonzalez claimed self-defense and was acquitted on charges of involuntary homicide. Brody was forty-two years old when he died.

4. ADRIAN ADONIS

A few weeks before Bruiser Brody was killed, Adrian Adonis died in a traffic accident. Adonis was one of four wrestlers traveling in Newfoundland, Canada, when their van swerved off the road, reportedly to avoid hitting a moose. Adonis died of multiple injuries that included a fractured skull and broken back. Two other wrestlers, Pat Kelley and The Wildman, also perished.

5. RIKIDOZAN

Rikidozan has been called the father of Japanese wrestling. During his career, he defeated such American greats as Lou

Thesz and Fred Blassie. In December 1963, his brilliant career ended when he was stabbed to death in Osaka, Japan.

6. RAVISHING RICK RUDE

Former Intercontinental champion Ravishing Rick Rude was forced to retire as a wrestler due to an injury in the 1990s. He was still active as a manager in 1999 when he died of a heart attack at age forty.

7. EDDIE GILBERT

Hot Stuff Eddie Gilbert was a popular wrestler and a former ECW tag-team champion. Gilbert succumbed to a heart attack at the age of thirty-four.

8. BRIAN PILLMAN

Brian Pillman shared the fate of Eddie Gilbert. Like Gilbert, Flyin' Brian had survived a serious car accident. Pillman was also a former tag-team champion. In 1998, the thirty-five-year-old wrestler died of heart failure.

9. HERCULES CORTEZ

Hercules Cortez teamed with Red Bastien to win the AWA tag-team title in 1971. Cortez was still a champion when he was killed in an automobile accident later that year.

10. CHIEF DON EAGLE

Chief Don Eagle was a favorite of wrestling fans during the 1950s. In 1966, the forty-one-year-old committed suicide.

Finishing Moves

L et's end this book with a list of some of professional
wrestling's best finishing moves.

1. THE WALLS OF JERICHO

Chris Jericho has never been one for understatement. He
turned the Boston Crab into his signature move, The Walls
of Jericho.

2. THE FRANKENSTEINER

Scott Steiner took the huracanrana, a staple of Mexican
wrestling, and renamed it The Frankensteiner. The monster
of a hold won the Steiner Brothers many matches and several world titles.

3. THE RUDE AWAKENING

Many wrestlers attempted to defeat Ravishing Rick Rude, but
few were successful. They were in for a Rude Awakening, the
name of Rude's put-away move.

4. THE DIAMOND CUTTER

Diamond Dallas Page owes much of his success to his finishing move, The Diamond Cutter, his variation of the DDT. What makes Page so dangerous is that he can execute the hold in almost any situation.

5. THE DISHONORABLE DISCHARGE

Col. Payne dismisses his opponents with his own version of The Diamond Cutter, appropriately named The Dishonorable Discharge.

6. THE RINGS OF SATURN

Perry Saturn forces wrestlers to tap out with a submission hold called The Rings of Saturn.

7. THE PEDIGREE

When Hunter Hearst Helmsley entered the WWF, he was presented as a Greenwich, Connecticut blueblood. He named his finishing move, a front face-lock pile driver, The Pedigree.

8. THE GRAHAM CRACKER

Johnny Graham, a light-heavyweight star in the 1990s, finished off his opponents with a sweet move called The Graham Cracker.

9. THE TORTURE RACK

Lex Luger's backbreaker lives up to its name of The Torture Rack.

10. THE SCORPION DEATHLOCK

Sting's finishing move is a Boston Crab renamed The Scorpion Deathlock.

Bibliography

BOOKS

Albano, Lou, and Sugar, Bert Randolph. *The Complete Idiot's Guide to Pro Wrestling.* New York: Alpha, 1999.

Gagne, Verne, and Melby, Jim. *Mat Wars.* Chicago: Contemporary Books, 1985.

Hofstede, David. *Slammin.* Toronto: ECW Press, 1999.

Hunter, Matt. *Wrestling.* New York: Smithmark, 1999.

Kay, Tommy. *Wrestling Book.* Scottsdale: Jalart House, 1974.

Morgan, Roberta. *Main Event.* New York: Dial Press, 1979.

Napolitano, George. *Wrestling, The Greatest Stars.* New York: Beekman House, 1987.

Ricciuti, Edward. *Wrestling, The Official Book.* New York: Mallard, 1992.

Sugar, Bert Randolph, and Napolitano, George. *The Pictorial History of Wrestling.* New York: Gallery, 1984.

——. *Wrestling's Greatest Grudge Matches.* New York: Gallery, 1985.

MAGAZINES

Ciacciarelli, Stephen. "Who's Who in Wrestling, 2000,"
  Wrestling World (August 2000): 7–86.

Lenker, David. "The PWI 500," *Pro Wrestling Illustrated*
  (Winter 1996): 19–61.

———. "The PWI 500," *Pro Wrestling Illustrated* (Holiday 1998):
  39–77.

———. "The PWI 500," *Pro Wrestling Illustrated* (Holiday 1999):
  39–77.

Welsh, Jack. "Commissioner Takes Bull By Horns," *Wrestling
  Revue* (July 1974): 20–24.

Index

About the Author

Floyd Conner is a lifelong football fan and the author of eleven books. His sports books include *Baseball's Most Wanted, Football's Most Wanted, Day By Day in Cincinnati Bengals History,* and *This Date in Sports History.* He also co-authored *Day By Day in Cincinnati Reds History* and the best-selling *365 Sports Facts a Year Calendar.* He lives in Cincinnati with his wife, Susan, and son, Travis.